VALUE AND THE MEDIA

Göran Bolin is one of our most complete analysts of culture. He is a truly interdisciplinary scholar. In this pathbreaking volume, Bolin interrogates one of the key questions of our time – what is value? Transcending the existing terms of this debate, he offers new way forward, synthesising theory and research in a remarkable way.

Toby Miller, author of *Television Studies*

Value and the Media
Cultural Production and Consumption in Digital Markets

GÖRAN BOLIN
Södertörn University, Sweden

ASHGATE

Published by
Ashgate Publishing Limited
Wey Court East
Union Road
Farnham
Surrey, GU9 7PT
England

Ashgate Publishing Company
Suite 420
101 Cherry Street
Burlington
VT 05401-4405
USA

www.ashgate.com

British Library Cataloguing in Publication Data
Bolin, Göran.
 Value and the media: cultural production and consumption
 in digital markets.
 1. Value--Philosophy. 2. Cultural industries--Social
 aspects. 3. Digital media--Social aspects. 4. Mass media--
 Social aspects.
 I. Title
 302.2'3'01-dc22

Library of Congress Cataloging-in-Publication Data
Bolin, Göran.
 Value and the media: cultural production and consumption in digital markets / by Göran
Bolin.
    p. cm.
 Includes bibliographical references and index.
 ISBN 978-1-4094-1048-5 (hbk) -- ISBN 978-1-4094-1049-2 (ebk)
1. Cultural industries--Social aspects. 2. Value. 3. Mass media and the arts. 4. Popular
culture. 5. Digital media. I. Title.
 HD9999.C9472B65 2011
 384'.041--dc22

                                                                        2011009460

ISBN 9781409410485 (hbk)
ISBN 9781409410492 (ebk)

Printed and bound in Great Britain by the
MPG Books Group, UK

Contents

List of Figures and Tables

Figures

Tables

Acknowledgements

Many people have commented on early versions of this book, as presented at conferences over the years. They are too numerous to mention here, so I will settle with a collective thanks to all of those who commented on my work on those occasions, especially at the ICA conferences in Montreal, Chicago and Singapore, the *Media in Transition* conferences in Boston in 2007 and 2009, the ECREA conference in Hamburg in 2010 and the *Transforming Audiences* conferences in 2007 and 2009 in London, and especially to Annette Hill for inviting me to these conferences and offering me a visiting professorship at the University of Westminster in 2006, which provided me with time to develop thoughts presented in this book (and at her research seminars). I would like to extend more specific thanks to Staffan Ericson, Stina Bengtsson and Johan Fornäs for commenting on specific parts of the text, to Ekaterina Kalinina for sharing her library of fashion studies and to Peter Jakobsson and Fredrik Stiernstedt for discussions on digital markets. I also want to thank Nick Couldry for continuous discussions on value and field theory. Lastly, I would like to thank Judith Rinker for checking my language.

The work on this book and some of the empirical work behind it has been directly financed by a grant from the Swedish Research Council, but the research it builds on has also been financed the Bank of Sweden Tercentenary Foundation and the Foundation for Baltic and East European Studies. Language editing has been financed by Södertörn University. For providing me with this funding, these organisations have my sincere thanks.

I also want to express my sincere gratitude to Taylor & Francis for the generosity in letting me use parts of what has been published under their copyrights. Three articles have been 'remediated' in this book. In Chapters 1 and 2, I have incorporated sections from 'Symbolic Production and Value in Media Industries', *Journal of Cultural Economy*, vol. 2(3): 345-61, 2009. Chapters 2 and 6 also include a few sections from 'Notes From Inside of the Factory. The Production and Consumption of Signs and Sign Value in Media Industries', *Social Semiotics*, vol. 15(3): 289-306, 2005. In Chapter 5, I have re-used sections from 'Digitization, Multiplatform Texts, and Audience Reception', *Popular Communication*, vol. 8(1): 72-83, 2010.

Last, but far from least, I want to thank the six girls that I value the most, for just being there: Stina, Lisa, Vera, Rut, Mina and Marta.

Introduction

This book is a way of summarising the research I have conducted over the past two decades. This research has spanned several areas, from my PhD studies in the early 1990s (a media ethnography of young boys and their engagement in the amateur production and consumption of horror and action films, videos and fanzines) over research projects on television production (mostly entertainment, but also news and actualities), mediated spaces in shopping malls and other public and semi-public spaces and the use of mobile phones, to the analysis of branding and advertising (not least nation branding) and much more.

This somewhat unfocussed behaviour, rushing from one area of research into something completely different (as John Cleese would put it), undoubtedly has its downsides. An obvious risk is that the knowledge produced is broad but lacks depth. One knows a bit about many things, within many areas of study. However, despite the apparent empirical and methodological fragmentation, I would say that there are some constant theoretical features that I have carried with me through all these research projects over the years.

When John Cleese acted as a shifter between sketches in the television series *Monty Python's Flying Circus* (1969-1974) by announcing 'And now for something completely different', this was a way of binding together two sketches that were themselves self-contained, in the meaning that a pun in the one did not build on knowledge of the other. However, although the different sketches within each show did not comprise a narrative whole but were, just like a news broadcast, additive in their narrative structure of individual segments, they did have a specific kind of humour, a recurring gallery of characters, and a specific tone in their dialogue. I would like to think of my research career in the same way, whereby the seeming disparity of empirical focus is held together by a consistent approach and theoretical perspective. The relationship between cultural production and consumption is this theme, and within the framework of this thematic can be found a set of empirical phenomena, a specific theoretical perspective, and a range of conceptual tools connected to this perspective. Value is such a concept.

This book is about value. More specifically, it is a book about value and media – not necessarily new media (as is often assumed in discussions about value today), as one of the main arguments of the book is that the principles of how value is created, and how we as individual subjects value things, objects and practices, share many similarities between new and old media. This is not least so because the 'pre-digital' media – the book, the photograph, the phonograph, film, radio, television – are today subsumed under the process of digitisation, just as, of course, the media that were 'born' digital are. Naturally there are new and often quite specific features in value generation in connection to the rise of new media, and I will point these out in the course of the argument. But it is important to note, along the same lines as Thomas Streeter (1996), that there are principles of production (of value) laid out within the old media technologies that are still active and valid for the new media. This fact is usually forgotten, and the argument in this book is that because of this we need to historicise all contemporary phenomena (cf. Jameson 1981). This means that the film swappers I studied two decades ago (Bolin 1998), who produced amateur films and fanzines in the pre-digital era, share many characteristics and features with file sharers, videogamers, youtubers, facebookers, twitterers and other agents in the production and consumption circuits of digital media. They were also producing and consuming culture at a historical moment when technology changed the conditions for media production by being appropriated in creative ways in reception and use. A main argument in the book is that we need to acknowledge these differences between old and new media, but that we also need to acknowledge the principal similarities in the production of value.

When the concept of value is used in everyday parlance it most often refers to economic worth, but at times also to moral values. In relation to media and cultural production it is most often the former that is presupposed, although at times, especially in relation to specific kinds of controversial content such as pornography or violence, moral aspects are brought forth. However, there are obviously other forms of value involved in media production and consumption. Journalists often refer to news value as the quality of specific events that make them qualified for journalistic interest. Recently the European commission introduced the Public Value Test, which is an attempt to control the European public service broadcasters in order to keep them from making damaging intrusion onto the commercial markets for broadcasting. A public value test is 'a way of weighing public value against market impact', as the BBC writes on their web pages.[1] It is thus a value that stands in opposition to economic value. These are but two examples of non-economic value forms.

Increasingly often, cultural, aesthetic, social and other forms of value are only judged as positive if they contribute to economic value. The different cultural sectors of society are legitimated on the grounds that they help regions, cities, etc., prosper economically, that they are drivers of economic growth (which is seen as the ultimate goal of every society). Thus one should not be surprised to see cultural successes being appropriated for commercial reasons, such as when the international success of Swedish author Stieg Larsson's Millennium trilogy is considered beneficial to 'the Sweden trademark'.[2]

In 1998 Swedish Minister of Commerce Leif Pagrotsky initiated a special prize for best music export, awarded to Nina Persson of The Cardigans at Grammisgalan, the annual special awards event of the Swedish music business.

---

1   BBC: http://www.bbc.co.uk/bbctrust/our_work/new_services/ [Last accessed 27 January 2011].

2   'Nya Milleniumvågen. Varumärket Sverige stärks när Hollywood tar sig an Stieg Larssons succéböcker', in *Dagens Nyheter*, 21 August 2010, p. E3.

Around the time of the show, great hopes were held for the export of music and its contribution to Sweden's import/export balance (see Fleischer 2009).

The institutionalisation of this can also be exemplified by the Swedish research council The Knowledge Foundation (www.kks.se), which since its inception in 1994 has specifically directed resources to research that contributes to economic growth and entrepreneurship. In this subsumption of creativity and cultural activity in general to the market, concepts like 'sustainable growth', 'the experience industry', 'cultural entrepreneurship', etc. are flourishing. The aim is to speed up the processes of 'post-industrialisation'.[3] This is indeed a far cry from the 'culture industry' as debated by Max Horkheimer and Theodor Adorno (1947/1994) in the 1940s.

The same trend can be found in Norway, for example, where the Research Council of Norway, the main funding body of Norwegian research across disciplines, published a special thematic publication called 'Value creation' (Verdiskaping).[4] The examples can be extended to the reader's country of choice.

Although it might seem as if all kinds of value become subsumed under economic value, there are, to repeat from the above, also other value forms in society. This book is an attempt to argue the importance of such different forms of value in and of themselves, as legitimate sectors of evaluation irrespective of whether they contribute to economic worth or not. In other words, this book is an attempt to argue the autonomy of each field of value creation.

As consumers we constantly value different cultural items and artefacts, we bestow on them affection, care, worship and admiration; but also, in the negative, we loathe certain things and practices, despise them, laugh at them. Another recurrent theme in the book, then, is the relationship between value in exchange and value in use, as Adam Smith (1776/1991) would put it.

Value in media (and other) production is frequently discussed in terms of either value in use or exchange, in terms of political economy. But there are also other ways of understanding value, ways that stem from anthropology, and as value as *symbolic* exchange. Another recurrent theme in the book is the relation of these two principles of value generation to each other, as it is my argument that this is the key factor in understanding how value is created in both production and consumption. I will argue that value in relation to symbolic exchange actually highlights the connection between economic and moral values, with justification.

Value, it is argued in the book, is not an essence. It is always the result of an activity. Already the linguistic concept of value carries this duality of being both

---

3   See, for example, the publication *Aha Sweden. En industri utan skorstenar* (Aha Sweden. An industry without chimneys), KK-stiftelsen 2001, documenting the efforts of The Knowledge Foundation up to that time.

4   *Verdiskaping*, Norges forskningsråd, February 2010. Available to download from http://www.forskningsradet.no/no/Neringsliv/1244734249838 [Last accessed 31 January 2011].

a noun and a verb, both a thing and an activity, as can be seen in the distinction made in the *Oxford English Dictionary*, for example. We give value to something, and thus the thing becomes the value given to it (or negotiated). We agree on value, we justify value, and sometimes we de-value things in evaluative action. Irrespective of whether it is the result of work or of negotiation, value is the result of social activity, acted out in a social relationship. Value is produced relationally.

Another recurrent theme in the discussion on value in political economy, and perhaps more so in marginal utility theory, is that value is the outcome of rational processes (cf. Gagnier 2000). My argument is that this is inappropriate, or at least inadequate, for understanding how different kinds of value are produced. The generation of value is most often the result of irrational processes, of unforeseen circumstances, and of relations between various wills in social practice. This is not least so when it comes to media production, as much media production today is quite complicated – technologically, organisationally, socially and economically.

The aim of this book is to analyse value; the conditions under which it is produced, what it is phenomenologically perceived as, and how it works and affects media production and consumption. The contribution I would like to make is to the theoretical discussion on value in light of contemporary changes within the media industries. Value, then, is both an empiric object of study and an analytical tool. By this I mean that I want to both use value as a concept to unpack some of the phenomena related to contemporary media production and consumption, as well as explore how value is used by those involved in practices of production and consumption.

Chapter Outline

I have tried to write this book as a successively elaborated argument, whereby in each chapter I build on my arguments and discussions on the previous ones. This means that I will refer back to previous chapters now and then, especially to empirical examples but also to conceptual distinctions and theoretical arguments. It is certainly possible to select individual chapters and read them separately, but since there is cross-referencing between chapters I have privileged a linear approach to the book.

In Chapter 1, I will paint the general background to my argument, and point to the key changes or developments within the media and culture industries over the past few decades, with special attention to processes of marketisation and digitisation. I will also give a brief introduction of my main conceptual tools, and provide preliminary definitions for them. I have already said that the concept of value, which is at the centre of my attention, is used here as both an analytical category and an object of analysis, and therefore especially this concept will be discussed. However, I will also introduce other relevant concepts, including text, audience, production, consumption, media and culture industries.

In Chapter 2, I will introduce, explain and discuss my analytic model in more detail. This model builds on the field model of Pierre Bourdieu, and I will discuss the strengths and weaknesses of Bourdieu's version of the model (for example, Bourdieu 1993) and some of the criticism raised against it (for example, Hesmondhalgh 2006, Benson 1999, Couldry 2003), and will then, with the help of these critical remarks, elaborate on the model to fit my own purposes.

In Chapter 3, I will further develop the discussion on how contemporary culture and media production is organised, with a specific focus on how the industry has adopted new – and sometimes not-so-new – business models. I will argue that the workings of 'new media' have a great deal in common with how the old, broadcast mass media worked. However, I will also point to some new features in these business models and how they can help us better understand the directions in which contemporary culture and media production is developing. This discussion also involves questions of ownership (the legal forms, struggles over copyright and format rights, etc.).

In Chapter 4, I will focus on labour as one important feature of, and key to understanding, contemporary media culture. This involves special attention to the relationship between consumers, users and producers (and will naturally also draw on contemporary debates on prosumers and produsers, user-generated content, crowdsourcing, etc. See for example, Brabham 2008, Bruns 2008 and Hartley 2009). The chapter will start with a discussion of the two active audiences theorised in political economy and cultural studies, and how the activity of media users actually is beneficial for the media and culture industries.

In Chapter 5, I will focus on the specific character of the contents produced within media industries, and how content in the form of works and texts also relate to the changes in business models discussed in Chapter 3. I will discuss the general consequences on textual expressions in multi-platform environments, for example the limits of texts in a world where television and film extend into the social web, and where narratives are combined over platforms (most notably television/film and the web and mobiles).

In Chapter 6, I will develop the discussion introduced in the previous chapters, to explore the ephemeral nature and quality of the objects and commodities that circulate in media and cultural production. Here I will especially take account of processes of digitisation, how they have affected the cultural industries, and the commodities at the heart of these industries: that is, texts and audiences, but more lately, also internet traffic as a commodity. I will discuss these as sign commodities, and I will especially point to those instances in which digitisation has restructured and radicalised media commodities, and how this contributes to the economic valorisation process.

In Chapter 7, I will return to the concept of value and try to sum up my argument and possibly contribute to a further understanding of how value works in contemporary culture and media industries. I will also return to my analytic model, and evaluate its relevance for the analysis of fields of cultural production and consumption.

A Note on Data and Method

As this book is a way of summarising two decades of past research, an attempt at thinking beyond the immediate results and conclusions of my previous research in order to develop a comprehensive argument from that experience, this naturally means that I will also build on arguments and themes introduced, explored and discussed in previous publications of mine. In the continuous flow of the text, I will reference these publications, not least in order to provide examples that are often described and analysed in more detail there.

Over these two decades in my various projects I have engaged in a range of methodologies, from ethnographic approaches to media users, over interviews with media producers and executives, to quantitative analysis of statistical data on audiences, as well as textual analysis of various media content. I have not burdened the text in this book with lengthy accounts of data and methodology, and refer to my previous publications for details. I will, in the chapters that follow, give examples from these previous studies, shortly presenting them in the context that they were produced as I go along.

Chapter 1
Media Production and Culture Industries

In the late 1930s and 1940s, leading theorists of the Frankfurt School in exile in the US (Theodor Adorno, Max Horkheimer, Leo Lowenthal and others) were intensely engaged in the debate over the consequences of capitalist media and cultural production on cultural objects and art. Perhaps the most renowned example of this discussion is the culture industry essay that Horkheimer and Adorno published in 1947 (Horkheimer and Adorno 1947/1994), just a few years after it had been written and first circulated as a copied typescript in 1944 (Peters 2003: 60). The main concern of these two philosophically trained European scholars was the perceived transformation of cultural objects under capitalism, whereby the market logic and standardised production supposedly changed the meaning and function of art objects for their users. To Horkheimer and Adorno – as well as Leo Lowenthal (1961) in his writings about the emerging market for literature – this was an inherent feature of capitalism: The constant pressure for profit accumulation was the drive that forced the industry to seek new markets and new areas of production.

Naturally, the theory of the culture industry has been met with various kinds of criticism. Firstly, it has been criticised for being too elitist and one-sidedly negative, and for downplaying any attempts at resistance to the forces of capitalism (this criticism has been put forth not least from within Cultural Studies, where it has been likened to Althusserian Screen Theory; see for example, Fiske 1987: 93).

Secondly, it has been criticised for homogenising the culture industry into one sector. While Horkheimer and Adorno thematised their object of analysis in the singular, many have pointed to the reductionist effect of this and rather used the concept of culture industries in the plural. In the late 1970s, scholars such as Bernard Miège (for example, 1979) did this, and more self-consciously, David Hesmondhalgh (2007: 15ff) has argued for the use of industries in the plural, since each sector of media and cultural production lives under different production conditions, and hence their logics vary at least within the framework of capitalist production. This is also my position, and just like Hesmondhalgh I will use the term in its plural form. Patrik Wikström (2009: 12ff) argues that a more appropriate term would be copyright industries, but to me this seems like a narrowing of the field of analysis a bit, since – as I will show in more detail later – some of the culture industries have a very ambivalent relation to strong copyrights, and do not actually earn their revenues from copyrighted commodities.[1] I will also term this

---

1 Wikström's book is called *The Music Industry*, in the singular, and one can indeed ask oneself whether this is one industry or several.

sector the *culture industries* rather than *cultural industries*, on the grounds that these are industries for the production of culture and cultural artefacts. *Cultural industries* would rather imply a cultural dimension of the industrial production. There are, of course, such dimensions in various companies and enterprises, but this is not the focus of my discussion.

Thirdly, some have pointed out that although the culture industry might be a useful term, this industry has some very special features that distinguish it from other industries for commodity production. In an article with the illustrative title 'Theodor Adorno meets the Cadillacs', Bernard Gendron (1986) has argued along these lines, referring to both the Cadillac automobile as well as the doo-wop group with the same name. A major point in Gendron's argument is that the analogy between the production of 'functional artifacts' (the car) and that of 'textual artifacts' (the song) should not be drawn too extensively. I concur with this criticism, and will in later chapters discuss more thoroughly the respects in which the media and culture industries differ from the production of other commodities and objects (since not all media production results in commodities). This is not to say that there are no aspects of standardisation and rationalisation connected to the production of cultural artifacts such as songs and musical pieces. The point is rather that the types of standardisation of intangible commodities are different from those of tangible objects. I will develop and deepen this discussion in Chapter 6.

A fourth criticism can be mentioned, which, rather than forefronting the dominance of the culture industries, sees them as arenas for creativity and innovation. Hence, one speaks rather of creative industries that actively involve users and consumers in the production process, for example through user-generated content (see for example, Hartley 2005 for a representative collection, and Cunningham 2009 for an international overview). I will deal with this discussion in more detail in Chapter 4, but suffice it to say for now that the perspective on creativity fits my purposes less well, as it so one-sidedly focusses on individual activity and less on structural constraints. It is my position that we need to take both these aspects into account; that is, both individual agency and structural frameworks for that agency. Structural constraints are most often socially produced, and we will need to take this into consideration as well. As David Morley (1992: 275f) argues, macro structures can only be reproduced by micro processes (cf. Morley 1997: 126f).

Lastly, there have also been attempts to update the culture industries perspective. Scott Lash and Celia Lury (2007) take issue with Horkheimer and Adorno and argue that we have reached a new phase of global culture industry (in the singular). In doing so, they contrast the 'old' culture industry that was dominant from the 1930s through the 1970s with the new 'global culture industry'. The difference, they claim, is that cultural objects were previously determined, circulating as identical objects, while today the objects (which I would rather call commodities) are undetermined and 'take on a dynamic of their own' (p. 5). I would say that this is not so much a change that has happened to the object/commodity, but rather a change in how research has come to evaluate the object/commodity. If there is one thing that reception research (even uses and gratifications research from way back in the 1940s!) has taught us, it is that audiences/customers are (and always have been) using commercial commodities in unpredicted and plural ways (that is, unpredicted by the culture industry). However, although this fact is not new, what could be argued is that representatives of the culture industry today do not care about how the commodities are used (to put it bluntly): As long as commodities circulate on the market, the reasons they do so are of little importance to the producers or right-holders. To me this is a distinction that Lash and Lury do not make in their book, and thus overstate the newness of the culture industry.

Lash and Lury try to make a similar move when they distinguish between the 'classic culture industry', which was supposedly 'dialectical', and the 'global culture industry', which is considered to be 'metaphysical' (p. 15). I think this is a matter of confusing ontology with epistemology; that is, confusing *what is* with *what is regarded as*. And I do not believe Adorno – if we could ask him – would agree that the culture industry of his day was 'dialectical'. He might rather say that he analysed it dialectically, but that is a different thing altogether.

So, I have used some space to discuss the argument of Lash and Lury, because their departure is similar to mine (something has indeed happened with the circulation of commodities and objects), and they are fascinated by the same phenomena. They also focus on value, although they use this concept undefined in a somewhat vague way, somehow using the concept of value as a floating signifier that is adopted in very loose and pragmatic ways.

However, and to be fair to their writing, there are also parts that resonate with my analysis: for example, those parts that deal with brands (see also Lury 2004, Arvidsson 2006). I will return to this discussion in later chapters of this book.

An ideological shift also occurred in the debate. While the culture industry concept was adopted to describe a negative development (or at least an ambivalent one – admittedly, Horkheimer and Adorno's dialectical position also included utopia), today the industry metaphor is sometimes used in a celebratory fashion, and concepts like the experience industry, the creative industry, etc., are used by policy-makers as a positive value. In political rhetoric, the cultural and experience industries are often regarded as emerging market sectors, to be developed to reach more overarching national economic goals. The change in discourse in cultural policy 'from cultural to creative industries' (Garnham 2005) is not a national phenomenon, as these are processes of discursive changes that appear internationally (Hesmondhalgh and Pratt 2005).

Marketisation

The culture industries perspective brings with it a focus on the relationship between capitalist economy and its development, and the consequences of the order of capitalist production for cultural objects and commodities. Thus processes of *marketisation* are at the centre of this theory, and we need to say a few short things about this process initially. Although media and cultural production have long been affected by capitalist market economy, this has occurred to varying degrees and in a variety of ways depending on the media form (print, broadcast and music media, film, art, etc.), as well as on which geographical, historical or national context you look at.

In Europe, for example, radio and television broadcasting has been organised quite differently from in the US, but also differently from in the Soviet Union. While the US radio and television were run commercially already from the start, the organisation in Western Europe was mainly in the form of Public Service Broadcasting (PSB) and in Eastern Europe broadcasting was under state control. Gradually, the strong public service broadcast institutions were met by commercial competitors, and by the end of the 1980s Europe consisted of a dual situation with strong public service *and* strong commercial broadcasters. This changed the overall broadcasting landscape and also affected the ways the public service broadcasters organised their content, with, among other things, an increased focus on scheduling (Ytreberg 2000).

The print media have also been organised differently in different parts of the world. Of course there is no such thing as public service newspapers (although many journalists regard themselves as working in the service of their readers), and the main form of organising newspapers has been through subscriptions and advertising. An exception to this is naturally in nations under dictatorship, where the control over newspapers is in the hands of the state. In modern democracies, however, the main business model has been subscriptions or the selling of individual issues, in combination with advertising (see, for example, Gustafsson 2009 for a discussion on the ratio between these two forms historically). Indeed, the print media and the press have also changed due to changes in media technology (for example, the growing importance of the Web) and in the advertising markets, the rise of free newspapers (for example, *Metro*), and an increased emphasis on niche audiences to meet demands from advertisers.

The music industry has developed more refined means of distribution and marketing, as has film production. New ways of distribution in the form of streamed content have surfaced for both film and music, some of which build on new business models by which content is free and revenues come from advertising. In Sweden and six other European countries, the music service Spotify (www.spotify.com) launched such a service in 2008, which has been met with considerable success among listeners.[2] The service also comes in a 'premium' version, without breaks for advertising and with better sound quality and some other features that are not included in the advertising-based version (for example, the ability to use the service through an application on your smartphone). A corresponding service has

---

2   It is estimated that there are around 10 million users in the seven countries in which the service is available (besides Sweden, Spotify is also present in Norway, Finland, the United Kingdom, the Netherlands, Spain and France). Of the total number of users, 750,000 subscribe to the paid premium version (see *Dagens Nyheter Kultur*, 9 December 2010, pp. 2-3).

been developed in Sweden for the distribution of film – Voddler (www.voddler. com) – but has not yet reached the same degree of popularity although it was launched as early as 2005.

Another general trend that has made its mark over the past few decades is that media commodities are often coordinated across media forms and genres, so that a film is released together with its soundtrack, a computer game, etc. In such ways, the markets for cultural commodities have become integrated.

However, far from all cultural production is organised on commercial grounds. Many countries have subsidy systems in order to balance the commercial pressure on cultural production. Just to mention Sweden as an example, there are subsidy systems for the press (to uphold a plurality of newspapers), film production (the Swedish Film Institute) and the Swedish Arts Council (Statens kulturråd, www. kulturradet.se), whose task it is to 'implement national cultural policy determined by the Parliament' by allocating 'state cultural funding to theatre, dance, music, literature, arts periodicals and public libraries, and to the fine arts, museums and exhibitions'. In addition, one could consider the public service system within the broadcast media as being included in the national cultural policy in Sweden, although it is not financed via taxes but rather licence fees (also determined by the Swedish Parliament), just as it is in the UK and several other European countries. However, it is also true that these systems at times have been under fierce attack and questioned on neo-liberal grounds with the argument that culture should be economically self-supporting. The debates on and the organisational forms of the subsidy systems naturally vary between countries, but wherever they appear, they counterbalance the economic logics of cultural production.

A related tendency in late modern commercial production, generally, is that commodities have symbolic or semiotic qualities that add to their economic (exchange) value. The increasing emphasis on design and brand names has complicated the way we can understand the valorisation of commodities in media as well as other commercial production. Beginning in the late 1950s, economists such as John Kenneth Galbraith (1958/1964: 145ff) pointed to the increased emphasis on marketing and advertising, and the problems it posed for traditional economic theory. This was further elaborated on by Jean Baudrillard (for example, 1970/1998; 1972/1981; 1973/1975), who introduced the concept of 'sign value' as a complement to the traditional concepts of use and exchange value. The basis for this was a perceived shift in the production-consumption circuit, whereby the symbolic dimensions of material commodities became more important for the circulation of commodities in society. The importance of signs for the organisation of production within the culture industries is undisputed, and arguably, sign value has always been a major component of cultural commodities. However, today many (if not most) cultural commodities *are entirely made of signs*, produced through signifying practices.

Although marketisation as a process has a long history it also comprises some prominent new features, most notably the increased importance of sign qualities, but the production of culture has also increasingly become subsumed by other ends, and cultural commodities and events are increasingly being produced not to bring revenue in themselves but rather to market other things, even nations. Take a phenomenon such as the Eurovision Song Contest, broadcast since 1956 on European public service television (that is, for non-profit motives). When Estonia became the first post-communist country to win the competition in 2001, and accordingly was to arrange the final in 2002, they hired the British PR agency Interbrand for a project called Brand Estonia, with the ultimate aim to effectively brand the nation in connection to the cultural event, especially to attract foreign investment and tourists as well as increase the awareness of Estonia in the eyes of the world more generally. Through this strategic move the Estonian government used the Eurovision Song Contest as a form of cultural technology to promote Estonia, and to market it to the world (for a fuller account, see Bolin 2006 and, extending the example to the commodification of India, Bolin and Ståhlberg 2010). When such a mix of stakeholders meet in cooperative efforts, each representing different spheres and interests in society, there will also be a mixture of value forms involved – political, economic, social and cultural.

Digitisation

The development within commodity production towards increased marketisation and an emphasis on sign qualities can be said to have been intensified with the technological development of *digitisation*, the process whereby media texts are broken down into digits and are hence reproducible without a loss of quality. But digitisation not only simplifies reproduction; It also affects distribution since digital media texts become much easier to disseminate to customers, as the examples of Spotify and Voddler above indicate. As texts become more easily spread from producers to customers, they also become more easily shared between media users. This fact puts pressure on record and film production companies to develop more refined tools for the restriction of markets in order to secure future profit through copyright legislation – the debate around file-sharing being a case in point, as file sharing does not involve 'tangible carriers' for the textual commodities (cf. Wallis et al. 1999: 7). However, copyright is only applicable to (artistic) works, and accordingly other techniques of market restriction have been developed for other symbolic commodities like television formats or fictional characters in literature, film and popular culture in general (trademark) (cf. Gaines 1990).

The need for such legal techniques has also increased as digitisation allows the same basic narratives to be distributed via several different technical platforms. We may think of this as a shift on par with the one noted by Walter Benjamin (1936/1991) in his essay on the fate of art in the age of its mechanical reproduction, and see digitisation as another stage in this process, with qualitative consequences for the cultural object at its centre. Indeed, digitisation has led to important shifts in the ways commercial value is generated. Along with this process a need has arisen for the industry to regulate, but so has an increased need for more refined 'means of consumption' to enable audiences/readers/users to use digitised texts: When commercial commodities circulate in digitised form we need complex software and hardware to 'decode' the digits into accessible, consumable form. In order to download a film we need a computer, access to high-speed Internet, and appropriate software to be able to take part in or consume it, and thereby realise its value (Bolin 2005).

George Ritzer (1999) used the concept 'means of consumption' to describe theme parks, shopping malls and related spaces of consumption. I would, however, rather reserve the term for the technical gadgets needed by media consumers to read media texts – television sets, computers, MP3 players, portable DVD players, mobile phones, etc. The difference between Ritzer's and my uses of the term is thus between the means needed for the purchasing of (tangible) consumer goods and the means needed for consuming (intangible, symbolic) texts. These are means that appear at different points on the production-consumption circuit.

Several attempts have been made to understand the effects of digitisation and new means of consumption for the generation of economic value (for example, Oberholzer-Gee and Strumpf 2007). There are also quite a few studies on the use of digital commodities and objects, especially downloading (for example, Blomqvist et al. 2005). The general results are inconclusive, not least due to the difficulties involved in estimating economic gains or losses (Lucas 1999, Kretschmer et al. 2001, Rosén 2008). However, there are few studies on the effects of the general processes of production and how they relate to the production of other kinds of value besides the economic ones (but see for example, Ross 2000, Kenney 1997). In relation to television production, I have elsewhere analysed how the value of being 'public service' can be struggled over, and how the political and cultural connotations of this concept have been used as a competitive field strategy by the commercial broadcaster TV4 in Sweden (Bolin 2002, 2004b). As already stated, public service production further complicates these things as it competes with commercial production on the one hand, and on the other hand does not strive for maximum profit.

As Thomas Streeter (1996: xi) argues, 'the legal and political problems facing computer communications today are much less unique and much more associated with broadcasting than the oft-heard euphoric rhetoric of "the information revolution" would imply'. This will be also my standpoint in the following, and I will draw to some extent on examples from television production and the commodities and objects produced there as 'electronic intangibles' (ibid.), from a European perspective of the dual structure of public service and commercial television production.

Convergence

A buzzword that has appeared as a consequence of digitisation is *convergence*. Although the concept dates back to long before the advent of widespread access to personal computers and broadband, it first became a buzzword with the full impact of widespread digital access. But it was already a concept in the early 1980s, when political scientist Ithiel de Sola Pool used it in his *Technologies of Freedom* (1983). Referring to the technical capabilities of the media as blending into one another, as de Sola Pool did in his book title, is obviously the most common way convergence is used. As with all widespread words, a concept's meaning drifts, and we are soon equipped with a number of ways to use it. This has naturally been observed by many scholars, and there are quite a few overviews of the many meanings of convergence (for example, Storsul and Stuedahl 2007, Jensen, 2010). For my purposes, the two main dimensions of the concept are those of technological convergence and institutional or market convergence.

By *technological convergence* I refer to processes in which media technologies, including technological platforms as well as networks of communication, are interconnected through production, distribution or reception. By *institutional integration and market convergence* I refer to the ways different media markets that were once separate are merging today. Media markets in themselves are, of course, nothing new. With the advent of a mass medium such as the book a market also appeared, with publishing houses and people with special skills with working procedures connected to these. However, since printing was the only available media technology, there were no other sectors that could be integrated. Since then, new media have continuously appeared, adding new markets in relation to them. So, from the longer historical perspective a plurality of media markets has gradually appeared, specialising in their respective genres tied to specific media technologies: the industries of publishing, newspaper, film, radio, television, etc. These media markets are, at present, being integrated. This integration does not always follow from the digitisation process (we can only think of the integration of film and television, cf. Wasko 1994), although this process has certainly speeded up the development.

In this process of market convergence, media companies formerly in different media branches join forces, which leads to institutional convergence. On the organisational level this has led to a situation in which media organisations that had previously concentrated on a specific medium, say print, such as Bonniers in Sweden and Schibsted in Norway, have today developed into media houses that are moving into other sectors like the broadcast media, the film industry, etc. These kinds of tie-ins have, of course, long been observed by scholars within the field of political economy of the media (for example, Herman and McChesney 1997), but are increasingly hard to ignore even for those more interested in media aesthetics and media reception, since these relations have effects on the construction of media content (and hence also have a bearing on media reception), as I will explore in greater detail in Chapter 5.

A Note on Historical Perspectives

Above, a brief account is given of the main changes in the culture and media industries throughout the 20th century. A few words should be said about such historicising accounts and the consequences of focussing too hard on change, developments and even media revolutions. An oft-made claim is, for example, that contemporary media systems have grown increasingly complex, and that production and consumption in late digital modernity are hard to grasp. Complexity, of course, is a rhetoric device, often adapted as a legitimising feature for making social or cultural analysis. However, the notion of increasing complexity, the feeling that we indeed live in complex times, is a recurrent theme in social and cultural analysis, at least since the first half of the 20th century. Accordingly, one can find this quote in one of the major works of urban anthropology from the 1920s:

> [w]e are coming to realize, moreover, that we today are probably living in one of the eras of greatest rapidity of change in the history of human institutions. New tools and techniques are being developed with stupendous celerity, while in the wake of these technical developments increasingly frequent and strong culture waves sweep over us from without, drenching us with material and non-material habits of other centers. (Lynd and Lynd 1929: 5)

In media and cultural research there is thus a tendency to emphasise the present changes, and one is often oblivious to the fact that previous generations of researchers have experienced the same evolving processes of change. This sometimes leads to an over-emphasis of the effects of the contemporary changes, and to an experienced need to throw all previous research out the window in favour of paradigmatic shifts in approach and conceptualisations. To give but one example, one could say that the concepts of mass communication and mass media today seem outdated, to the benefit of personal media and from within the media industries, me-media, etc. In Chapter 3 I will discuss this in more detail, but suffice it to say for now that there is a profound risk of throwing the baby out with the bathwater by being oblivious of previous processes, and there is a profound risk that one will end up re-inventing the wheel.

On a more general level, one could rather say that the notion of living in constant change is a founding experience of modernity, where 'all that is solid melts into air', as Marx and Engels put it in *The Communist Manifesto* (Marx and Engels 1848/1888; cf. Berman 1982/1988). Researchers and cultural debaters sometimes forget about this, and overstate the changes at hand. This is not to say that nothing is new under the sun, but one should be sensitive to the distinction between those phenomena that are genuinely new and those that are just re-heated dishes from yesterday's cuisine – albeit perhaps with a new topping or added spices.

Marx's theory of history, most elaborated on in *The German Ideology* (Marx 1932/1995), as well as theories of modernity more generally, view history as a linear process. Linear historiography naturally privileges the unfolding of history as a series of events that are causally bound together, so that one act leads to another. Theories of modernity typically emphasise linear advancement and progress (and sometimes decline), and Marx's historical thinking was obviously a typical example of history unfolding in developmental stages.

Historical perspectives, however, need not necessarily build on linear apprehensions of events. Admittedly, there are several ways one can look upon the past. The linear perspective is perhaps the most common view on history, but it might be fruitfully complemented with the punctual, non-linear perspective of history as points in time, which can be connected to one another through similarity in kind. This is the view famously suggested by Walter Benjamin in his famous 'Thesis on the Philosophy of History' (Benjamin 1955/1999). Benjamin's example is the French Revolution, during which the ancient Roman Republic stood as a historical model, as 'a tiger's leap into the past' (Benjamin 1955/1999: 261; cf. Peters 1999: 3f). The metaphor of the tiger's leap is today perhaps mostly used in relation to the future, for example through the idea that one can jump stages in the historical development of media technologies. In relation to mobile phones it is sometimes called 'the leap-frog hypothesis' and is mainly used in trying to understand historical processes, like the one in several African countries whereby landline phones have never been established and mobile and wireless telephony are being instituted from the start (Howard 2007).

This dual perspective on history can be most useful when one wishes to understand phenomena that appear at different points in time and are marked by similarity rather than causality. It can indeed shed light on practices that repeat at intervals of several years, and help us to see seemingly new phenomena in light of old ones. One could, as I will do in more detail in later chapters, ask why certain kinds of do-it-yourself practices emerge in society at different points in time. These practices can go under different headings (DIY, amateurism, enthusiasm, fandom, or user-generated practices), but the principles behind these practices might be the same, as might the societal context in which they appear.

Value

Philosopher Douglas Magendanz (2003: 443f) claims that the concept of value is indefinable, just as is the concept of truth. The reason for this is that value, just like truth, 'represents a series of ramifying concepts', and among a range of such concepts he mentions 'belief'. If we consult the *Oxford English Dictionary*, we find *value* defined as that 'amount of some commodity, medium for exchange, etc., which is considered to be an equivalent for something else', the 'material or monetary worth of a thing', a 'standard of estimation or exchange'. Or, again in the words of Magendanz (2003: 443), an 'agreed or assumed standard, criterion or measure'. *Value* is also both a verb and a noun; That is, it is both a concept referring to an activity and a concept referring to a 'thing' or a phenomenon.

Value as verb and noun is naturally connected: A thing *is given* a value, and hence *also becomes* the value it has been given or valued. Value is thus produced socially in that we, through our interpretation of objects, actions and phenomena around us, give them meaning in a socially and historically defined space. Standards, measures and criteria are *agreed* on, disputed over and negotiated in social interaction. Agreement on the standards or criteria for judgement does not imply that everyone arrives at the same evaluative conclusion. But when there is agreement on the principles of judgement, a discursive space is opened for struggles over which interpretation or evaluation of the thing, person or action is the most valid (cf. Frow 1995: 19).

As has been pointed to by John Guillory (1993), the concept of value has its 'origin in the eighteenth-century discourse of political economy', where it was introduced 'in the struggle to distinguish art from the commodity' and fundamental in the distinction between use and exchange value as theorised by Adam Smith and David Ricardo, and is later picked up by Karl Marx (Guillory 1993: xiii). The connection between the economic and the cultural is therefore at the heart of processes of evaluation and value judgements. Value is constructed socially, but, as Marx (1867/1976) argued, the social process results in the fetish character of the commodity whereby the social processes (of work for Marx, but here extended to the social process of evaluation) become hidden in the commodity form as (exchange) value – the accumulation of which becomes capital. Capital is thus an asset, something that can assume many forms (money, estate, etc.) and can also be converted between these forms.

Marx dealt mainly with the production of material commodities and objects. As a consequence, both use and exchange value in Marxist thinking are the results of raw material, means of production and labour. Exchange value is the value that is realised when the commodity is circulated on a market and sold for a price that can be turned into surplus value, later to be reinvested in the production and ideally turned into new surplus value. However, as sign value has become more important in the generating of exchange value it adds an element of complication to this process, as prices on markets are becoming increasingly arbitrary. The absence of raw material in commodity production, and its intense dependence on labour, makes the price-setting mechanisms more diffuse for consumers, as it is has bases other than the raw material that is tooled into artefacts. When products are composed of digits labour becomes even more important, as 'the commodity, then, is only as good as the labour that goes into it', as Tiziana Terranova (2000: 48) puts it. Another way to phrase it is that the production of non-tangible commodities becomes more dependent on the *belief* in the commodities' specific value by customers, since there is no comprehensible material base for it. The belief systems surrounding the design components in the production process are thus of crucial importance.

Belief is also the central component in fields of production, according to Pierre Bourdieu (1977/1993). Belief in the value at stake in the field – the value struggled over, which is the motor of the field dynamics, is the ultimate product of the field. This means that the production of belief is also the production of value. Cultural producers naturally always justify their production in one way or another. If there is a belief system, there will also be arguments for its justification, according to principles worked out in the field (principles and criteria of evaluation, for example). As Luc Boltanski and Laurent Thévenot (1991/2006) have argued in their broad analysis of such principles of justification in various social circumstances, justification is one of the foundational modes that drive social action, and is as such complementary to Bourdieu's field model.

So, when we look at the production of digital non-tangible commodities, it is apparent that there are other kinds of value circulating in the production than mere economic ones, and that these other value forms also have an impact on the (economic) valorisation process. Television production, for example, as a special and very transient form of non-tangible commodity production, is surrounded by a number of intersecting interests and objectives on the part of the agents involved, which all have a bearing on each other and influence each other's value-generating efforts. Technologically and administratively complicated, television production involves a range of individuals and organisations: broadcasters, production companies, advertisers and sponsors, and the individuals who inhabit these organisations but whose activities cannot all be expected to have similar personal aims (Bolin 2002). That television production (at least in Europe) can be divided into public service production not aimed at producing surplus value, and commercial production, which has this kind of production as its final goal, complicates this even further.

In fact, television production lends itself well to exemplifying the complex web of value forms that are drawn into late modern cultural production, not least since it is also, as pointed out by Streeter (1996), an early form of production of intangibles that precedes today's dominant form of intangible digital production. But there are naturally also other forms of intangible commodity production that are of concern for the analysis in this book, such as music, news, social networking, film, etc. Just like television production, film production involves many interested parties, from individual creators like directors, scriptwriters and actors to other film workers who are more anonymous (see, for example, Caldwell 2008, and, for industrial perspectives, Miller et. al 2001 and Wasko 1994), all of whom are important for the end product but whose names in most cases are not typically known to the general film viewer. The same can be said about print news production, whereby the general reading public is for the most part unaware of who the original author of each single news feature is (although journalists typically believe that everyone reads newspapers in the same way as a journalist does, keeping track of the individual behind each news story).

In the next chapter I will elaborate on Bourdieu's (1992/1996) field model of cultural production, to make it better fit the analysis of media and cultural production. Since Bourdieu's main focus was the production of acclaimed art and literature, he had rather little to say about mass or popular culture other than as a means of depreciation in the struggle for social power in fields of restricted production (see, for example, Bourdieu's [1983/1991] article 'Did you say popular?'). In order to be of value in the analysis of less consecrated texts such as most of those produced by the media and culture industries, one needs to develop and adjust Bourdieu's field model, and I will build further on my previous discussion of the field model in Bolin (2004b), and on other qualifications and critical remarks made by Benson (1999), Couldry (2003) and Hesmondhalgh (2006).

Texts and Works – Audiences and Users

One of the major results of media production is texts. These texts, however, can take on many different shapes and forms. The concept of text can also be used in a narrow or a more inclusive sense, as those webs of meaning that we interpret, engage in and sometimes produce ourselves as media users. Because media production also presupposes that there are people who interpret and engage in texts. This might be due to several reasons, but there are very few people who produce texts for no-one to read.

It is of course commonplace in contemporary media studies to define texts not only as written texts but also in the wider sense as woven webs of meaning. However, if we want to be more precise we might want to adopt the distinction between work and text introduced by Roland Barthes (1971/1977). The work, according to Barthes, is 'a fragment of substance, occupying a part of the space in books (in a library for example), the Text is a methodological field' (p. 156f).[3] This means that the work is that combined unit of signs that can be attributed to an author, for example *Ulysses* by James Joyce (1922/1946), *The Girl with the Dragon Tattoo* by Stieg Larsson (2005/2009), *La Strada* by Federico Fellini (1954) or *Berlin* by Lou Reed (1973). This distinction will have consequences on how we can think of commodities in the digital, user-generated era, in which media users become increasingly involved in textual production (but more seldom in the production of works). For now I will make this distinction, and will hence refer to *works* when I discuss identifiable narratives that can be attributed to an author and that are fixed in some recognised medium, and to *texts* when I discuss more fluid webs of meaning. Naturally, works can relate to various forms of representation involving images and sounds in fixed or moving form. With digitisation, these works need not necessarily be bound to a single platform of presentation. On the one hand they can appear in basically the same form on different platforms, the paradigmatic example being a cinema feature film that can appear on television with the same narrative unfolding but on a smaller screen and in another reception context (but it can also, of course, also be specifically edited for television). On the other hand, works can involve several technical platforms, such as when stories for small children who cannot yet read are combined in a book with a CD, which can be considered an early form of 'transmedia storytelling' (Jenkins 2006), a concept I will return to in Chapter 5.

As works are bound to some platform of representation, but through digitisation can also float between different platforms, they are, in their commodity form,

---

3   Barthes capitalises 'Text' throughout the article, whereas he obviously does not ascribe 'work' the same importance.

often called immaterial commodities, for example inscribed in judicial discourse as 'immaterial rights', 'immaterial property', etc.[4] I will try to avoid this conceptualisation as digital artefacts and commodities do have a material form: Electronic impulses through cable networks, and indeed light flowing through fibre optic cables, also have a physical materiality in the form of physical energy. However, we cannot put light or electronic impulses in our pockets without the use of means of consumption and distribution, and in this respect digital commodities are intangible. So, rather than using the concept of immaterial commodities, I will speak about intangible objects.

Sometimes in media research, the concept of audience is used to describe readers of works (and sometimes also co-producers of texts). However, as Vincent Mosco and Lewis Kaye (2000: 45) have argued, the concept of audience was born in 'the marketing departments of companies with a stake in selling products through the media'. Hence, audience is the commodity circulated within the production-consumption circuit of media industries. This commodity should be separated analytically from the social subjects that take part in, interpret and enjoy (or indeed loathe) media texts. For these social subjects I reserve the concepts of *readers*, *listeners* and *viewers*, or, most of the time in order to include the activity component of that agency, I will use the concept of *media user*.

A few words should also be said about the concept of medium, especially as used here as media production and consumption. If we define a medium as any technology that can be used to communicate, then basically everything can at one point or another be used as a medium. However, such a broad definition would also render the concept meaningless. Klaus Bruhn Jensen (2010: 64ff) has made a distinction between such technologies as 'media of three degrees', whereby media of the first degree are tied to bodies and their extension in tools', such as language (speech) and writing (p. 66). Media of the second degree include 'printed books and newspapers to film radio, and television' (p. 68). Jensen then goes on to describe media of the third degree, by which he means 'meta-technologies' like the digital computer and mobile phone (p. 69f).

Jensen's account of media of three degrees has a strong base in 'medium theory' in the wake of Harold Innis (1951), Marshall McLuhan (1964) and Walter Ong (1982). A limitation of medium theory of this kind is that it is very technologically focussed, and gives less attention to the ways the media in society are organised. So, in the following when I write of media production, I wish to refer not only to communication technologies but also to institutional forms. These institutional forms can be formal (as in mass-media companies within film, radio, television, advertising and public relations, record companies, book publishing, computer games enterprises, etc.), but they can also be more informal, such as those that are self-organised within social networks or fan communities. In line with David

---

4   In Swedish the corresponding concept is 'immaterialrätt', which directly translates to 'immaterial rights'. It is thus also inscribed in legal discourse on a global scale. See Humphreys (2008) for a discussion.

Hesmondhalgh (2007: 13), I exclude some aspects of the culture industries (the theatre, musical productions, etc.), not because they are uninteresting from a culture industries perspective – clearly the musical business is not (see, for example, Jonathan Burston's [2009] interesting analysis of the Broadway musical), but because they will not add much to my analysis. However, the art business is seldom considered part of the culture industries, but as art is often counterposed with popular culture, art exists in a dialectic relationship with mass or popular culture, and it is therefore necessary to bring up art production at times.

The relationship between art and mass or popular culture has been intense and wide-ranging over the years. This is not the place to engage in this discussion in its entirety, but I do wish to make my position clear at this point. Firstly, it is commonplace in contemporary debates from the 1980s and onwards to argue that the lines between high and low cultural forms, or between art and mass/popular culture, have – if not dissolved altogether – at least become blurred (for example, Frow 1995, Laermans 1992, Collins 1989). While this might have been a politically motivated move in the 1990s in order to legitimate the analysis of popular culture texts and practices around them, it appears less interesting today (and it is quite possible to argue that there has always been a blurred boundary between these spheres of value). In line with Staffan Ericson's (2004: 11ff) very nuanced analysis and discussion of the will to dissolve the boundary, I hold the continuous struggle over this boundary and the ways it is constituted as more interesting than its possible upheaval.

The explanation for why this boundary has appeared has also been a major focus of attention over the years. A common apprehension is that modernist art and avant-garde aesthetics have developed as a reaction to the mass or popular commodities produced by the culture industries. So argue, for example, Leo Lowenthal (1950/1957) and Dwight Macdonald (1595/1957) as well as Peter Bürger (1974/1984) and Andreas Huyssen (1986). To these thinkers, artists constantly have to find new expressions at the pace the old expressions becoming commodified or popular in terms of being liked by the many. The causal explanation offered by these authors is that mass culture arises as a consequence of the general industrialisation process, and artists then have to change their production.

There are, however, other explanations. Hungarian philosopher Sandor Radnoti (1981) pointed to the fact that the division between high and low art forms was already present before industrialisation and the mass cultural commodity. According to Radnoti there is something suspicious about the homogenisation of 'the concept of mass culture', the tendency to make all mass cultural commodities alike:

> The assumption of the unity of the mass culture is just as much an ideological construction as the absolute generalization of the market, and it is needed precisely for the purposes of another ideological construction: the self-definition of the concept of art. (Radnoti 1981: 33)

To Radnoti there is a dialectic relationship between art and mass culture. They define each other:

> [T]he concept of high art is not merely a theoretical reflex of a culture in the process of capitalization, not simply a response to the commodification of art and its rationalisation in terms of profits – even though it is this, too – but rather the conceptual integration of those mechanisms as a precondition for the unification of the 'free rational arts'. (Radnoti 1981: 33)

In this statement Radnoti does not reject the idea that artists strategically distance themselves from commercial mass culture ('it is this, too'). But he sees this in light of another move: the construction of the unified mass object, which becomes the antithesis and definer of the opposite object: the art object, and hence artistic practice.

With this move, Radnoti acknowledges the relational character of the production of art and the production of mass or popular culture. This relational thinking also opens for analogies with other relational thinkers, such as Pierre Bourdieu and his field theory. In the next chapter I will discuss this theoretical framework in terms of an analytical model, but it is important to note already at this point that this relational analytical model cannot write out any part of culture production, neither art nor mass or popular production.

This means that I will also use a similar relational perspective when more generally discussing the concepts of production and consumption. It is common parlance in media studies to speak about media consumption. However, it is far from always clear what is meant by this. Sometimes in media theory, media consumption is accounted for as synonymous with media use (for example, Ang and Hermes 1991, Morley 1995, Silverstone and Hirsch 1992/1994). However, if we are to use the concept of media consumption in any meaningful way, it has to stand for something other than just 'watching television' or 'reading the newspaper'. We need to qualify the specific circumstances in which it is fruitful to think of media users as consumers, and when it is better to use other descriptions (citizens, for example). Consequently, I will reserve the concept of consumption for discussing media (and other) use that is involved in a circuit of production and consumption. I will discuss the relationship between production and consumption in more detail in the next chapter, but would like to signal this already at this stage.

***

This chapter started with an account of the relevance of a culture industries perspective on the present changes and conditions within media and culture production and consumption. I have briefly outlined my points of departure and the traditions of research I wish to contribute to. I have also briefly indicated some of the themes I will discuss and give more empirical substance to later in the book. Connected to these themes are a bundle of concepts such as value, text, work, object and commodity, etc., which I will naturally also return to in later chapters. The reader should bear in mind that my ultimate aim is to try to understand how value is produced in media and culture industries, and how specific frameworks of production, involving a mixed set of interested parties involving commercial and non-commercial agents make this value-generating process quite complicated, but also more interesting.

In the next chapter I will discuss and outline in more detail a model for the analysis of production and consumption in media and culture industries. This model is based mainly on the work of Marx, Bourdieu and Baudrillard, and will be put to use in subsequent chapters.

Chapter 2
Fields of Cultural Production and Consumption

To most people, the obvious outcome of media production is probably media works: novels, television programmes, music pieces, news features, cinema films, computer games, etc. And when we think of media consumption, we correspondingly think about how we consume media content. In the previous chapter it was concluded that works today, with the advent of digitisation, have become increasingly freed or separated from their tangible carriers. In the pre-digital era, most works were bound to material form: a shellac record, a book, a newspaper. All these could be bought by media users, who could posses, trade or exchange them in the tangible form they were given in the production process. Some of these works could come in various tangible forms, for example books, which have long been available in both hardback and paperback form. Some books also originated from series in newspapers, which is another form in which a narrative could be distributed to readers. And, eventually, music also came to be distributed via several technological platforms. The hit song from an LP could also be bought as a single (and sometimes in a special remixed version), later also on tape, and now increasingly in non-tangible form as a digital tune that can be downloaded to a computer, MP3 player or mobile phone, or as streamed content accessible online. In their digital appearance, works, then, are not platform-specific.

However, some works already at their first appearance are not possible to privately own in this way (at least not for the ordinary media user), for example a movie at the cinema; You cannot bring it with you when you leave the theatre. What you bought as a cinema visitor was the opportunity to experience the work, not the work itself. And what you brought with you when leaving the cinema was the experience of having taken part in a cinematic narrative. Today most works have this quality, since digitisation can be said to have liberated texts from the industrially defined platforms of the pre-digital era. Most works, however, need to be decoded through increasingly advanced digital means of consumption, but the media user has a certain freedom to choose exactly which means of consumption he or she will use, as well as the reception context. The restrictions concerning this are less technological than economic, and depend mostly on what and how many different consumption technologies the media user can afford.

Media production is, naturally, part of the wider field of cultural production in society. In this chapter, I first wish to elaborate a bit on such fields of cultural production, in order to then relate these to fields of consumption. It is often argued that the boundary between production and consumption is dissolving with the advent of new digital technologies, which provide ordinary media users with tools for production. This is naturally true: the means of consumption is most often also the means of production. One example is mobile phones, with which we can consume bandwidth while talking, texting and surfing, but which also provide us with the means to take pictures and record moving images, sound, etc., and furthermore, together with a computer and relevant software, bring with them the possibility to manipulate (edit) what we have recorded. And, needless to say, they also provide the means of distributing the results of our productive efforts. The same goes naturally for computers, whereby the ability to produce is not so much dependent on hardware as on which software one has access to. Much of this production is, however, outside the market economy. It does not aim at making profits, and it is initiated on various grounds, including the sheer fun of exploring one's creative abilities, making an impression on one's friends or family or passing the time while waiting for transportation or a friend, and it is often not thought of as valuable in any sense. Nonetheless, it has consequences for industrial production, and this also means that there is a limit to the culture industries perspective, and its accompanying commodification thesis, in which economic value is emphasised (albeit implicitly in relation to other values). For this reason, I shall now widen the perspective and develop a model aimed at the analysis of fields of cultural production and consumption inspired by Pierre Bourdieu. In the first section of this chapter I will introduce Bourdieu's field model, first in terms of fields of cultural production, and then in relation to fields of cultural consumption, where I will try to modify Bourdieu's analytic model, partly with the help of Baudrillard and his concept of sign value. In the course of this I will also bring in two of the influences both Bourdieu and Baudrillard build on: the economic theory of Karl Marx and the anthropological theories of symbolic exchange of Marcel Mauss.

Fields of Cultural Production

Media and cultural production is, as noted in the first paragraphs of this chapter, part of the wider field of cultural production. The specific boundaries of such fields can, quite naturally, only be empirically defined. But suffice it for now to indicate that fields of cultural production include the production and evaluation of cultural expressions in symbolic form. This means on the one hand the production of art (including the performing arts), and on the other hand the production within the culture industries: journalism, music, literature, computer games, comics, etc.

The specific attraction of the field model is that it tries to capture the dynamic processes of cultural production, involving not only cultural producers in a narrow sense, that is, artists, authors, film directors, composers, etc., but also other agents surrounding these producers of cultural expressions: curators, critics, sponsors, cultural institutions (for example, museums, film festivals, book fairs) as well as prizes. The foundations of the field model of Pierre Bourdieu can be found

CE+ CC+

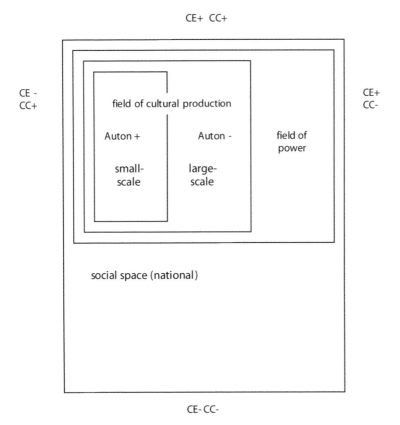

CE -
CC+

CE+
CC-

field of cultural production

Auton +   Auton -   field of
                              power

small-   large-
scale   scale

social space (national)

CE- CC-

CE Capital – Economic	Auton + High degree of autonomy
CC Capital – Cultural	Auton – Low degree of autonomy

Figure 2.1   The field of cultural production in the field of power and in social space

Note: Based on Bourdieu (1992/1996: 124).

in, for example, *The Rules of Art* (Bourdieu 1992/1996). This model was in fact developed in articles over several decades beginning in the 1970s, some of which are translated and published in Bourdieu 1993). In *The Rules of Art*, Bourdieu discusses the field of cultural production as a specific (sub)field of the larger field of power, in turn a part of (national) social space (see Figure 2.1).

The structuring principle for the field of cultural production is the opposition between the degrees of acquired cultural and economic capital, and between the consecrated top positions of the field versus the not yet consecrated positions of newcomers, challengers and other agents who have not (at least not yet) acquired dominant positions within it. Thus, Bourdieu makes a distinction between the sub-fields of 'small-scale' and 'large-scale' production, whereby the former consists of production for other producers, and is thus restricted in its kind. This part of the field is marked by its high degree of autonomy. Value judgements here are made solely on aesthetic grounds, and production is carried out for its own sake (*l'art pour l'art*), unaffected by outer demand and influences from other areas of social space. In the 'sub-field of large-scale production', production is directed towards an unrestricted market of undifferentiated consumers, and success is measured in widespread popularity and counted in economic terms. This part of the field is low in autonomy and, according to Bourdieu, has to obey the forces of the economic market.

There are at least three problems with Bourdieu's model. The first, as Hesmondhalgh (2006: 222) has pointed out, concerns the question of scale. Bourdieu labels the less autonomous part of the field of cultural production the 'sub-field of large-scale production'. However, there are many commodities produced in this part of the field that do not fit this description. A common misapprehension, for example, is that television broadcasters strive to reach as large an audience as possible. This model might have been the guiding light for broadcasters in the past, but today large audiences are considered a problem, as advertisers do not want to pay for audiences they do not want to address. In the eyes of advertisers who want to reach 17- to 25-year-old girls, all other viewers are 'waste', and are in this sense literally *worthless*. According to a production executive at Swedish TV4, the company has ceased charging advertisers for audiences over the age of 55, and has started to 'give them away for free' (cf. Bolin 2004b: 283). This is also the main logic behind the fact that television broadcasters differentiate their pricing. Prices are set according to how well a certain television programme attracts the target group. As advertisers are interested in 'reducing wastage', an increasingly fine-tuned targeting of audiences arises. Techniques for this are attempted within the television ratings industries, but this is naturally easier to accomplish in digital environments, where each click confirms a media user contact.

Furthermore, within the music business, as Hesmondhalgh (2006: 225) points out, most records produced never recover their investment. Out of ten records, the popular story goes, nine fail. These nine artists, then, or records, seem to destroy rather than produce economic value. And, many of the most acclaimed artists of their time are actually economic successes (for example, Bob Dylan, The Beatles, etc.). So, how can we understand this in relation to the field theory?

The solution is, I believe, to be found in Bourdieu's theory of the production of belief (Bourdieu 1977/1993). The problem with the Bourdieuan terminology is that the concept of large-scale production privileges an emphasis on the scale of production, rather than its aim. The question of consecration is, then, not so much coupled with how many records (or books, paintings, etc.) you actually sell, but with *the way you relate* to your production. So, whether or not Dylan sells an infinite number of records is beside the point. His legitimacy depends on the fact that he *does not seem to care* whether or not he sells; That is, he is not aiming at achieving economic success. At least he convincingly appears to act beyond or above economic goals in his cultural production, and in this respect convinces his audience of his artistic autonomy. So, if one can convince others that one's motives for production are not economic but instead artistic, and can thereby produce an authentic aura as an artist (rather than as a profit-maker), one can get away with being economically successful. As this example suggests, it might be better to speak of sub-fields of restricted and un-restricted or heteronomous production, and altogether avoid concepts of scale.

The second problem is connected with the strong emphasis Bourdieu places on 'the two fundamental principles of differentiation – economic capital and cultural capital' (Bourdieu 1992/1996: 344). The opposition between cultural and economic capital, and hence between cultural and economic value, is certainly of great importance, but as has been pointed out by Rodney Benson (1999: 485), the opposition is also problematic. The emphasis on the dichotomous character of the structure obscures the fact that other kinds of value can be involved in the power struggles within the field. For example, non-commercial, public service television production cannot be explained by this model, as stakes are not made to produce profit and success is not measured in terms of economic value. Public service television is more reliant on the production of political, and perhaps also educational, values in order to gain legitimacy for its activities and secure broadcasting licence agreements (cf. Bolin 2004b).

A third problem is whether there is only one field of power in society, as Bourdieu suggests both in *The Rules of Art* (1992/1996) and in his analysis of French elite schools in *The State Nobility* (Bourdieu 1996). This problem goes unaddressed by both Benson and Hesmondhalgh, but is in my view a key explanation of the two other problems they mention – especially that of the dual opposition between the cultural and the economic. It is also unresolved in Nick Couldry's (2003) article on the media as producers of 'meta-capital'. With specific reference to Bourdieu's theory on the field of power in *The State Nobility* (1996), Couldry develops an argument in which he claims that the media, in the same way as the state, are in possession of a meta-capital that has strong influences on all other fields and hence on the value generation within those fields.

However, for all the merits of Couldry's article, and they are many, we are left with the same problem: Is it more helpful to regard the power relations as played out within one field of power or is it, as I suggest, better to regard the situation as constructed by several competing fields of power? Although the media are certainly – in the same way as the educational system – one of the most powerful agents of exercising symbolic power (that is, to produce naturalised representations of reality), the media do not – in the same way as the state – have the coercive power to *force* these representations upon other fields. In this respect it might be more helpful to think of the relationship between the field of media production and other fields of power as a web of interrelations.

If political value is produced within the field of political power, would it not be more productive to regard this as a separate field of power than to include it in a general power field? Furthermore, if there were one comprehensive field of power, that field would certainly not only be structured by high and low assets of economic and cultural capital. It is quite clear that Bourdieu's field model is inadequate for explaining relations between the most powerful agents in society even at the national level, as all these agents do not struggle over the same positions, and do not argue the same value judgements over the same objects and phenomena.

To solve this problem I would like to propose another model for analysing field relations in order to explain how several kinds of value are produced, especially those produced in the sub-field of undifferentiated and unrestricted media production.

One of the crucial factors that can account for the production of multiple value forms is the question of autonomy, and the relative dependence between fields. In Figure 2.1, autonomy is higher in the sub-field of restricted production, and lower in the sub-field of unrestricted production. This means that the value produced in the latter sub-field is more sensitive to influences from forces outside the field of cultural production. Bourdieu emphasises the economic as an explanation, and argues that the sub-field of weak autonomy is low on cultural assets and high on economic ones. However, I suggest that, although the forces of the economy are hard to neglect, at times there are other kinds of value that are influential to the value generation within the field of cultural production. I have tried to illustrate this in Figure 2.2.

In Figure 2.2 it is proposed that the economic power field is but one of the fields of power that are influential on the part of the field of cultural production with low autonomy. Indeed, for commercial media production, audience statistics and lifestyle analyses are of utmost importance – audience statistics are the 'currency' that works in this subfield, to use the terminology of the broadcasters. However, for public service television it is obvious that it is not primarily the commercial field that is important, but rather the political and perhaps even the educational or academic field of power (the field that governs knowledge value). It is within the power of agents in the political field to decide on licence rights and concessions charters for broadcasters such as Swedish SVT and TV4 as well as British Channel 4. This is also why it is important for public service broadcasters to engage in audience measurement, as this is the tool that can produce arguments that a company is fulfilling certain public service goals: to reach all citizens and not avoid elderly viewers, to provide for minority programming, etc. So, for public service broadcasters it is not mainly the economic field of power that is the main motor of outer demand and pressure on the field of cultural production. For these broadcasters it is rather the political field of power that formulates demands on this subfield of production, which explains why public service broadcasters also engage in audience measurement, with the same techniques as the commercial broadcasters, but with other aims and centred on other forms of value (although the jargon of the audience statistics as valid 'currency' reigns even there). This is sometimes commented on as a commercialisation of public service, but this need not always be the case. It is arguably not the methods of measurement that define what is commercial and what is not, but rather the value these measurements are turned into in the combination of audience statistics with arguments based in other

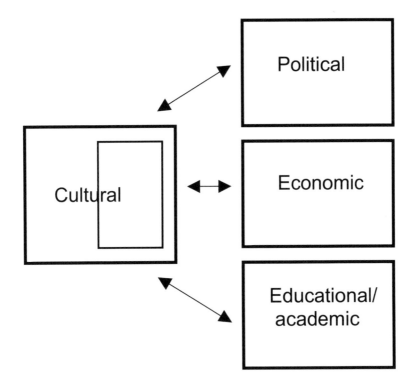

Figure 2.2   Outline of the relations between four fields of power

Note: This model has been discussed in an earlier form relating to the field of television production (Bolin 2004b), and is then elaborated on in relation to journalistic production (Bolin 2007b).

belief systems than that of the economy (for example, the social value forms of inclusion and general civic enlightenment).

Above I have tried to clarify my argument about the general production of different value forms (economic, societal, political) with examples from broadcast television in its commercial as well as public service forms. I have done so because the case of commercial and public service television is relatively straightforward compared to other forms of media production, as they obey outer demand from two quite clear spheres of power: the economic and the political. The basic argument that media and cultural production most often obeys outer demand from fields outside the field of cultural production is, however, also valid for other kinds of production, as I hope will become clearer in subsequent chapters. The economic field of power is naturally most often involved, but equally often in conjunction with other fields of power (the academic or political field, for example).

Adding to the complexity of this production is also ordinary media users, who, in Bourdieu's theoretical world, most often act in the field of consumption, which of course is related, but not equal to, the field of production. The specific relationship between the fields of production and consumption was never clearly accounted for by Bourdieu, perhaps because he did not find it important enough to investigate to its full extent (perhaps on account of his primary interest in the production of consecrated art rather than in less consecrated forms). It is my argument that the digitisation of cultural production, which makes it possible for media users to engage or interfere with the process of production, makes it important to further develop this relationship theoretically. In the next section I will therefore first discuss the dialectic relationship between production and consumption, in order to then relate the two fields to each other.

Fields of Cultural Consumption

That production and consumption are intimately interrelated was one of the main arguments in Karl Marx's theory of the commodity in the first chapter of volume one of *Capital* (Marx 1867/1976). In order to more fully understand the relations between the fields of production and the fields of consumption, we need to take a detour through this theory of the circulation of the commodity, as it (as I will argue more fully later) is fundamental in understanding the arguments of Bourdieu and, perhaps less surprisingly, Baudrillard.

In *Capital*, Marx distinguishes between, on the one hand, different kinds of production and, on the other hand, different kinds of consumption. People have always produced goods for themselves and for others, but this does not necessarily mean that everything produced is a commodity. On the contrary, much of what is produced by men and women is not. If we were to enter an ordinary school classroom, we would find a great deal of production going on. Smaller children might be making drawings of their pets, siblings or parents, and indeed, these drawings might be of value to their parents and other close relatives. They can be given away as birthday presents, to the appreciation of the recipient, but will very rarely become objects that will circulate on a commercial market. Thus, they are not commodities. They have *use value*, in that they are the result of work and raw material, and/or can satisfy human needs (that is, they are useful in some respect). A commodity, in addition to use value, also has *exchange value*. That is, it can be bestowed with an economic value on a market. The market is also the place where the relationship between the production of the commodity and its consumption is constituted. In order to close the circuit, commodities need to be bought by consumers, who use them for various purposes that might, or might not, be the ones intended by the producer. This is where the circuit is closed, and it is only at the moment of consumption that the commodity is realised in the process. In the realisation of the value of the commodity, in the process of consumption, the use and exchange values are destroyed. However, the commodity that has now been consumed can then have entered into a new production-consumption process.

Marx distinguishes between three kinds of production-consumption relationships. For instance, when producing a material commodity the producer needs to have raw material, for example a piece of wood in order to produce a chair. To this is added human labour to tool the material into the end product. In this production process, the raw material is consumed. This is what is termed *productive consumption*; In the industrial production process the raw material as well as the labour executed by the worker are consumed (see also the 1857 Introduction to *Grundrisse*; Marx 1939/1993). Productive consumption results in exchange value, that is, the difference between the costs of production and the economic value (price) that can be bestowed on the commodity on the market. Involved in the process is also *reproductive consumption* – the worker consumes food, clothes and other goods in order to reproduce his or her own work capacity. Machines and other means of production need to be tended to and kept in shape, parts changed, etc.

In a similar way it can be argued that all consumption results in the production of something, albeit not always commodities. When the individual television viewer, for instance, consumes a television programme in his or her leisure time, he or she produces ideas, meaningful discourses, views of the world and, in the long run and in combination with other things consumed, identities and cultures. The outcome of such consumption, however, is very seldom a commodity. You cannot sell your view of the world, and few people would be interested in buying your identity. These are obviously products produced in the consumption process that do not have a market. From an economic perspective this consumption is *unproductive*, as it does not contribute to the production of capital.

As has been noted by many followers of Marx, his theory privileged a focus on the production moment in the circulation of commodities – this was the point that was the determining factor for the other moments (distribution, exchange, consumption), and was therefore the driving force in the process. But beginning with the works of Jean Baudrillard in the late 1960s, a shift in focus can be observed. Baudrillard, in his re-readings of Marx, noted that in late modern society consumption had become more important for the process as a whole, and that it had become a duty, rather than a pleasure or a right, to consume (Baudrillard 1970/1998: 80; cf. Bauman 1998).

In a series of three books published in the early 1970s, Baudrillard argues that with the development of late modern capitalism follows a shift in the production-consumption circuit, whereby the symbolic dimension of material commodities becomes more important for the circulation of commodities in society (Baudrillard 1970/1998, 1972/1981, 1973/1975). With this Baudrillard introduces the concept of *sign value*, in addition to the Marxist concepts of use and exchange value. Sign value, however, is somewhat problematic as a concept (see also Murdock 2000). Although it is easy to see the point Baudrillard is trying to make – to highlight the increasing importance of signs and symbols in the production of economic value – it is not entirely clear from his writings how this value should be related to exchange value. Furthermore, although Baudrillard displays a strong interest in the workings of the media in society, he has surprisingly little to say about the specific kind of production the media are involved in, for example the fact that most of the objects and commodities produced are non-tangible in kind, and have the defining feature of being constructed out of combinations of signs.

To Baudrillard, sign value is the result of the development of the fetish character of the commodity (that is, the abstracted reified labour). If use value is the quality of the good (that is, that product that is outside the market economy) or the commodity, and the exchange value is the price set on the market for a commodity, then sign value is that value that gives status when it is consumed or spent. We could also speak of 'utility value, commercial value, statutory value' (Baudrillard 1972/1981: 125). Sign value is, then, involved in the production of difference, for example social difference. It is also, for Baudrillard, related and structurally parallel to exchange value. If, for example, I buy a car, it obviously has a use value for me: I can move between different places I need to be, say between home and work. But the car I have bought can simultaneously fill other functions. Any car would take me from my home to work, but it would make different impressions on my co-workers if I drove a Bentley or a Toyota. Seen in this way the sign value would be part of, and contribute to, the exchange value, that is, the economic value I am prepared to pay in order to choose the Bentley over the Toyota. This has to do with, on the one hand, sign values consumed in production, for example the fact that the seats are made of genuine leather, the dashboard is constructed of oak, etc. – all of which are signs of exclusiveness compared to the less exclusive materials used in other car brands. These are signs that, when turned over in productive consumption in the production process, contribute to the exchange value of the car when sold. On the other hand, sign value can also be extracted as a value in its own right in the act of realising its value in consumption: the value that differentiates me from other car owners, and the impression it makes on my co-workers. It therefore also has a relatively autonomous relation to exchange value.

However, these examples are mine, not Baudrillard's. Baudrillard is in fact quite vague when he discusses the relationship between sign value and exchange value, and he has even less to say about how sign value relates to use value. I will return to this relationship in the next section, especially the question of its role in production as well as consumption, but suffice it for now to say that sign value can obviously 'fulfill needs' in the Marxian sense, for example by giving pleasure of various sorts and kinds (cf. Maxwell 2001: 129ff), and in this capacity could be regarded as having use value.

Just like Marx, Bourdieu was most often engaged in analysing fields of production (and for the most part restricted production). His main example was the formation of the literary field in France at the turn of the last millennium in *The Rules of Art* (Bourdieu 1992/1996), in which he showed how the field was constituted, how authors and other stakeholders in the field navigated, and how the field also produced the literary forms at its centre. Although Bourdieu's main body of work dealt with cultural production, one could say that his most known work actually dealt with fields of consumption. In *Distinction* (1979/1989), he mapped the cultural tastes of consumers, and showed how taste functions as a marker of status, and that it is in fact a tool in the struggle for social power. Through taste and preference we indicate our positions in social space. The focus of Bourdieu's attention in this social space is what could be called the 'classifications game', in which social subjects evaluate and classify cultural objects and practices they are confronted with: food, drinks, art, fashion, music, literature, entertainment, leisure habits, and so on – and other social subjects in this social space, one should add. 'Taste classifies, and it classifies the classifier', as Bourdieu (1979/1989: 6) states in a famous passage of *Distinction*. This also means that we cannot avoid classifications, because the refusal to classify, the unwillingness to announce one's opinion in cultural matters will also inevitably be classified by others, so one is drawn into the game of classification and evaluation irrespective of whether one wants to or not.

In his analysis of consumption Bourdieu does not speak of fields, or fields of consumption, but rather analyses the distribution of taste in 'social space'. The principles of his analysis, however, follow the same logic of correspondence as his analysis of fields of cultural production, and I will hence in my argument use the concept of field of consumption in order to emphasise its structural similarity to the field of cultural production.

The field of production and the field of consumption are, then, structured according to the same principles, and the social struggle for, and marker of, power work according to the same mechanisms. However, and most importantly, the field of production and the field of consumption are separate entities. They are not the same, although they are interconnected. If there are changes in the principles of valuation in the field of consumption, say a certain artist becomes more popular among larger parts of the listening audience, this will have an effect on the field of production of which this special artist is a part. However, there is, as indicated above in the example of Bob Dylan, no automatic correspondence that dictates that growing popularity in the field of consumption leads to decreased status in the field of production.

In the next section I wish to elaborate a bit more on the relations between production and consumption, focussing on some of the distinctions made by Marx in his theory of the commodity and the production-consumption circuit, and especially emphasising the dialectic character of this process. I will also briefly indicate the consequences of the various parts involved in this circuit for the shift we are facing today towards an increased production of intangible commodities, of which audiences in the form of statistical aggregates is one.

From Productive Consumption to Consumptive Production

In the context of my attempts at relating fields of production to fields of consumption, then, we need to relate these concepts to the production-consumption circuit. If we consider the production side in the production-consumption process, we can easily find many examples of *productive consumption*. In the production of a television programme studio space, props, video tapes, electricity, film, etc. are consumed.

Newspaper production involves the consumption of paper, ink, photographs, etc. The production of music requires instruments, studios, electronics and recording equipment, etc. The specific tools thus differ between various areas of cultural and media production, but irrespective of the means used, there will be moments of consumption embedded in production, and in the process of this, raw material will be tooled, and sometimes worn out, contributing to the end product of the specific media industry. And just as the result of production can be an intangible commodity, intangible parts can also be consumed in the process of productive consumption.

Let me illustrate this with the example of the audience as a part in the production-consumption circuit. If seen from a production perspective, which undeniably is the main vantage point taken in the political economy of communication ('the phantom of production', as Baudrillard [1973/1975: 17] argues), audiences are the raw material that the media industries package in the form of statistics and sell to advertisers (who in turn sell this commodity to producers of market commodities) (cf. Mosco 1996: 148f). The audience is then a means for the producers of other commodities for creating surplus value in the form of profit to stockholders. In this process the audience enters into a new production-consumption circuit and is 'consumed' by the advertising industry.

This also explains why the spread of commercial television in Europe led to a re-organisation of audience research. In Sweden, for example, having had a public service monopoly in radio since 1925 and in television since the late 1950s, much research on viewers and listeners was conducted from within the public service organisation and their audience research division. In the early 1990s, with the introduction of commercial television companies broadcasting in Sweden, this division was disorganised, and the commercial audience poll enterprise Mediamätning i Skandinavien (MMS) started in 1992 (introducing people meters instead of telephone surveys, which the public service company had conducted).[1] With this shift, audience statistics on the reach and share of television and radio programmes changed from public information that anyone could access to private information, unavailable to the general citizenry (and media researchers, one might add), and sold for a price set by MMS. As an illustration of the structural similarities between the commercial and non-commercial production of the audience, many of those who had previously produced knowledge about viewing and listening habits for the public domain easily moved into the production of audiences as commodities.

The specific role of the audience in the production-consumption circuit has at times been analysed and discussed in media research. In an influential article Sut Jhally and Bill Livant (1986), strongly influenced by Dallas Smythe (1977),

---

1   MMS is jointly owned by SVT, MTG, TV4 and Kanal 5, all of which own 24 per cent each (plus two minor stockholders from the advertising business with two per cent each). Nielsen Media Research administrates the people meters in 1,200 Swedish households, comprising 2,600 people on the panel.

argue that what audiences actually do when they watch television is work for the television companies, adding human labour to the raw material (the commercial clips), thus producing surplus value for the television companies. A fundamental problem with this reasoning is that, besides the fact that it confuses statistics with real viewers, it is very hard to see what the audiences' wages are or what they get in return for watching. If work – as a concrete social activity that differs from the abstracted form, labour – is defined as those activities you get paid for by the owners of the means of production, then the individual subjects in the audiences seem to be working for free. It might be argued that what audiences get is television programmes, but if audiences are working, and if their salary is entertainment shows, how can they further convert this salary? The average viewer cannot buy food with the experience earned in watching an entertainment or any other television show. Few people besides media researchers and media critics can convert the knowledge gained from such shows into exchangeable commodities in the capitalist media market. It is then easier, from the perspective of Jhally and Livant and with the terminology of Marx, to claim that the watching of entertainment is part of the recreation of the worker's labour power. This recreation time is then refined, packaged and sold on a market by companies such as MMS. From this perspective the watching is certainly part of the media market system, although not as an activity that produces something, but as raw material for refinement in the production process *by others* (cf. Meehan 2000: 77). The labour of statistical production, then, ultimately results in commodities.

The labour of consumption cannot be characterised in the same way as the labour of production, although there are structural similarities between the two processes. This is also why it is important, at least from the analytical perspective presented here, to distinguish audiences (as commodities circulating on a market) from the social subjects that watch, listen or read, that is, consume media content. This distinction is important to make because audiences and media users are both engaged in the production-consumption circuit, but play different roles in it. The audience is an abstract category. It has no will of its own, and cannot act. It is an entity worked upon and refined into an abstract commodity on the market. It is raw material. This in contrast to the viewers, readers and listeners, who actively interpret media texts, in which process becomes produced meanings, identities, cultures. In this capacity the readers are also working, although not on the market for commercial commodity production. They are rather working in a field that aims at another end product – social difference and sign value. What we are confronted with here are two different factories (to use the industrial metaphor): One that produces audiences (that is, a commodity), and one that produces social difference (which is not a commodity). The labour in both factories is centred on signifying practices – practices that at times are drawn into the production-consumption circuit of the media and culture industries.

Furthermore, it is also sometimes the case that the use of the media by consumers can result in things that actually do feed into the production-consumption circuit in the form of contributions to media content. This is the process by which media users are not drawn in as objects (audiences) but rather subjects (media users), acting in a media environment that has increasingly provided users not only with means of consumption, but also – and at the same time – with means of production. These tools can be used for the production of works in the form of, for example, blogs, which might exist in commercial environments although they are (most often) not produced for the purpose of economic gain. Nonetheless, if published on commercially driven websites, they become part of the commercial activities anyway.

The mirror of the productive consumption of statistical audiences, to allude to one of the works of Baudrillard (1973/1975), might be called *consumptive production*. This refers to the process in which the act of consumption results in something other than just waste, that is, a new object or commodity that feeds into a new production-consumption circuit. This mirror of production is, however, not the same mirror Baudrillard discusses. His mirror is the lacanian mirror in which the 'human species comes to consciousness' (Baudrillard 1973/1975: 19), the reflected image in which we as humans recognise ourselves, in which we come into being, just as the child becomes aware and enters into its own subjectivity in the mirror phase, following structural psychoanalysis (that is, Lacan). The mirror I am referring to does not concern our subjectivity, but points to the dialectical opposite of production – its flip-side, if you will.

Above I have argued that – from the perspective of production – the audience as a statistical aggregate, a commodity that is tooled into being by the statisticians and strategists at the marketing departments of media companies, does not work, has no will of its own, and no power of agency, as opposed to the viewers, readers, listeners and media users who engage in media objects and commodities. From a production perspective audiences do not work, which is why Smythe, Jhally and Livant and others are mistaken when they say that audiences work for the media industries. However, from the perspective of consumption these viewers, readers and listeners, in their consumption practices, contribute to the production-consumption circuit, and from this perspective it is certainly a form of labour being carried out, the end product not being commodities but rather social difference, status and legitimacy. This social difference as produced in media consumption can, however, be tooled into a commodity, and enter into a production process. This is arguably what Facebook and other social networking sites do with user profiles, which are created by users but do not become a commodity until they are refined in the factory of the social networking site and tooled into a commodity sold to advertisers (as will be further analysed and discussed in Chapter 3).

According to Marx, the productive force needed to produce exchange value is human labour. The basis for this is that human labour can produce more than it takes to reproduce. If by analogy we look at consumption, we could argue that what separates human consumers from other consuming components in the production-consumption circuit is that humans can also consume more than it takes to reproduce the human consumer force. And this is actually what consumers do when they buy things that do not ultimately turn into use value for them (they never use them) – food is wasted, clothes are thrown away unused when we do a spring cleaning of our wardrobe, etc. These commodities, then, do not realise their value in use but rather in waste. Through over-consumption we fulfil the duty to consume, one of the products being waste. In this way, over-consumption also lubricates the wheels of late capitalist markets as it produces the need for new work tasks for those who have to take care of and handle waste – not least the electronic waste produced when we upgrade our means of consumption, for example by throwing away a perfectly usable mobile phone, just because we 'need' to have a new updated model, for instance the exchange of an iPhone 3 for an iPhone 4. As the slogan on Apple's web site goes: 'This changes everything. Again'.[2]

A machine involved in productive consumption cannot 'over-consume' in the same way as human consumers can. We can thus introduce *consumptive force* as a concept in pairs with productive forces. This is also how social and symbolic exchange value is produced from the needs of consumers, needs ultimately produced by the abstracted consumption homologous to abstracted work in the moment of production in the circuit. Consumption, then, results in the production of sign exchange value at the social level of differentiation between individuals:

> Hence, it is vain to oppose consumption and production, as is often done, in order to subordinate one to the other, or vice versa, in terms of causality or influence. For in fact we are comparing two heterogeneous sectors: productivity, that is, and abstract and generalised exchange value system where labor and concrete production are occluded in laws – the modes and relations of production; secondly, a logic, and a sector, that of consumption, which is entirely conceived in terms of motivations and individual, contingent, concrete satisfactions. So, properly speaking, it is illegitimate to confront the two. On the other hand, if one conceives of consumption as production, the production of signs, which is also in the process of systematization on the basis of a generalization of exchange value (of signs), then the two spheres are homogeneous – though, at the same time, not comparable in terms of causal priority, but homologous from the viewpoint of structural modalities. The structure is that of the mode of production. (Baudrillard 1972/1981: 83, n. 24)

It is not altogether clear why Baudrillard insists that the sphere of consumption is structured after the mode of production in the last sentence of the quote (he also both suggests and immediately abolishes the concept of consumptive force [or 'consummativity'/'consommativité' as he puts it in Baudrillard 1972/1981: 82]). If production and consumption presuppose each other, as was argued by Marx, why would consumption be modelled on production? Would it not be more helpful to see them as dialectical parts of the production-consumption process? Naturally, as is often noted, Marx privileged the moment of production. But it is

---

2   www.apple.com/uk/iphone, last accessed 16 December 2010.

harder to see why Baudrillard, in his criticism of Marx and his insistence on the importance of the moment of consumption, should repeat this bias. In line with dialectical thinking, it would seem more helpful to see them as equally important parts in a circuit, and this is also the perspective I will adopt in the following.

This ambivalence, however, might explain why some of the contemporary work on consumption, in which the consumer has been elevated to the 'global dictator' (Miller 1995: 1) in the world economy, has misunderstood Baudrillard's insistence on the importance of consumption. The confusion seems to lie at the level of the field of consumption, which has been mistaken for the individual consumers within it. But it might be more helpful to regard consumptive forces as part of the production-consumption circuit – a circuit which needs consumers to be equally free to set their power or ability to consume at the field's disposal, as workers need to be free to sell their labour power.

The Field Relations of Production and Consumption

Now, it might seem like a giant leap from the production-consumption arguments of Marx and Baudrillard to Bourdieu's field theory, and one might wonder if this detour over Marx has been necessary. On the one hand, it would be possible to argue that the political economy of Marx would suffice for the analysis of contemporary digital media environments. Or, the opposite, that Bourdieu would be quite enough, perhaps with the aid of Baudrillard. My point is, however, that there are severe limitations in both the political economy of Marx (and Baudrillard) as well as the field theory of Bourdieu. The political economy of Marx can only help analyse commodities circulating on the market, and as much media production is non-market motivated (Benkler 2006) Marx simply cannot account for this. This restriction is not tied to the field model, as it concerns all kinds of production irrespective of motivation. In fact, Bourdieu's field model presupposes a tension between the pole of restricted production, centred on cultural value and produced mainly in opposition to economic value, and the pole of undifferentiated, or perhaps more accurately unrestricted, production (as market differentiation and segmentation in fact make up a prominent feature of contemporary media markets), whereby economic value is the measure of success.

Furthermore, it is easy to see that Bourdieu is indeed more influenced by the Marxian theory of value generation than is generally acknowledged. This is understandable on the one hand, as he constantly refuses to label himself Marxist (or to adjust to any other label, for that matter). However, on the other hand he often returns to Marx in his theoretical discussions. One need only flip through the indexes of some of his early works to note the many places in which he refers to Marx, for example in his *Outline of a Theory of Practice* (Bourdieu 1972/1992), *Distinction* (1979/1989) and *Language and Symbolic Power* (1991). In interviews he is also often asked about his relation to Marx and Marxism, for example in the collections *In Other Words* (1990) and *An Invitation to Reflexive Sociology*

(Bourdieu and Wacquant 1992), and it is very obvious that he is well read in Marx's oeuvre.

The most explicit influences of Marxist theory in the field model are perhaps revealed in the widely cited article 'The Forms of Capital' (Bourdieu 1983/1986). Although Marx is not mentioned in either the text or the reference list (which, by the way, is not an uncommon way of Bourdieu to treat his influences), the concepts and discourse Bourdieu uses echo almost verbatim Marx's labour theory of value:

> Capital is accumulated labor (in its materialized form or its 'incorporated', embodied form) which, when appropriated on a private, i.e., exclusive basis by agents or groups of agents, enables them to appropriate social energy in the form of reified or living labor. [...] Capital, which, in its objectified or embodied forms, takes time to accumulate and which, as a potential capacity to produce profits and to reproduce itself in identical or expanded form. (Bourdieu 1983/1986: 241)

This quote in fact lies very close to some of the original formulations by Marx, for example when he writes that 'all commodities, as values, are objectified human labour' in *Capital* (Marx 1867/1976: 188). What actually differs between these two quotes is that Bourdieu argues that capital is accumulated labour whereas Marx argues that it is value that is the reified (and accumulated, one would presume) labour. We shall return to this variation in perspective later in the book, as the full penetration of this difference here will not add to our understanding of the relationship between the fields of consumption and production, but we can still bear in mind that although Bourdieu might be influenced by Marx he does not slavishly rehash his arguments.

In the introduction to the edited collection *Language and Symbolic Power* (Bourdieu 1991), the editor John B. Thompson (1991) briefly discusses Bourdieu's relation to Marxist terminology and argues that although there are obvious influences when it comes to the concepts used, these influences are on the level of approach, and Bourdieu does not so much adopt and use the conceptual framework in any un-reflected way but rather reworks it, and also does so in relation to influences from the sociology of Durkheim and the structural anthropology of Lévi-Strauss, the gift economy of Mauss and the phenomenology of the body of Merleau-Ponty.

The influence of Marxist thought in the field theory of Bourdieu is also accompanied by sociological and anthropological theories of symbolic exchange – just like Baudrillard's analyses of the political economy of the sign. By incorporating theories of symbolic exchange Baudrillard and Bourdieu transgress the theoretical framework of Marxism, which makes it possible for them both to extend their thinking beyond the mere economic. The basic inspiration comes from Émile Durkheim's *The Elementary Forms of Religious Life* (Durkheim 1912/2001), in which he developed thoughts on the sacred in society, thoughts later to be developed by Marcel Mauss in *The Gift* (Mauss 1925/1990). The theory of symbolic exchange is a theory on social relations and societal integration. The gift and the counter-gift are acts of communication and confirmation of social status, and have the dual status of being 'both positive communication and agonistic confrontation' (Merrin 2005: 14). Bridget Fowler (2006: 113), for example, summarises the theoretical influences of Bourdieu, describing his theory as 'partly an inventive elaboration of Marxist materialism', while simultaneously owing 'a line of inheritance from Durkheim's idea that men and women generate classifications of the world, doxa, which have their roots in social divisions, but which have a profound influence in the form of their basic beliefs about the social game'.

It is thus not hard to see the influence of Mauss in Bourdieu's analysis of the 'logic of social exchanges' (Bourdieu 1983/1986: 253) within fields of cultural production and consumption. Baudrillard's adaptation of symbolic exchange is a bit more complex, however, and although he expands and develops Marx's theory on the production-consumption circuit it is not always entirely clear how this affects the everyday production and consumption of signs and material commodities. But it is evident that he wants to seek an explanation for how value is produced (and which kinds are produced) that transgresses those presented by Marx. Bourdieu, who has to a much greater degree than Marx dealt with the production of other kinds of symbolic values that can be said to make up capital (although he also does not have much to say about the production of media texts), has developed his theory to account for how different kinds of symbolic capital (including economic) can relate to one another in the distribution and production of difference related to social life.

However, although it is easy to see the Marxian vantage point in Bourdieu's theory (as it is in Baudrillard's), it is also important to mark out the major differences. One of these is the view on value. If Marx sees (economic) exchange value as an objective entity, Bourdieu sees it as an *objectifiable* entity, in the sense that it can be objectified *in relation to* other values although not objectively measured in any way. Bourdieu, then, stresses the relational character of a value, and how it develops or transforms over time (and under the hands of labour and the structures of the field of which it is a part). But, equal to Baudrillard, Bourdieu emphasises the symbolic or non-material features of commodities and their ability to function as distinctive when consumed. And even more importantly, Bourdieu provides us with a tool for understanding how symbolic capital (economic, social, cultural) is generated as an effect of the relationship between the structures of the field, and of the agent's actions.

The basis for Bourdieu's theory is that value is produced as an effect of the relationship between agents and institutions in a social field. A field consists of the struggle between agents and institutions over a value, or capital, which is considered worth striving for. The value is simultaneously produced as a result of this struggle. In Marxist terms, one could say that the activity of struggling is the labour that produces the value. This value is specific to each field, each with its own institutions for evaluation and consecration. In a field of production, the art field to take Bourdieu's main example, there are consecrating instances (art critics, museums, art journals, etc.), positions (acknowledged artists, curators, etc.) and a value (art). The art field consists of four opposing poles: On the north-south axis there is the opposition between legitimate and illegitimate art (between consecrated artists and newcomers who have not yet advanced within the field, or who have not succeeded in attaining any legitimate positions). On the east-west axis there is the opposition between restricted and unrestricted production. The most consecrated positions are found in the restricted, legitimate north-west sector of the field.

The field of consumption is structured in a similar way. This similarity lies in the fact that the processes of judgement are the same (although they need not result in the same evaluations) (Frith 1991: 105). This means that the principles for the accumulation of value are also the same.

However, regarding the hypothetical example above that stated how the sign value of a Bentley would help produce difference between me and my co-workers, we need to acknowledge that this difference is in fact not produced in the field of production; It is rather produced *in another field*, that is, the field of consumption. Just as economic profit is the result of the ability of the owners of the means of production to take advantage of the fruits of production (the unrestricted part of the field of production where success is measured in economic value), the cultural gain at the centre of the field where difference is produced, results from the ability to make *a differential profit* by way of consumption. This differential profit can be reached in two ways: either by consuming quantitatively (having a multitude of cars, hundreds of shoes, etc.), or qualitatively (consuming only very refined culturally prestigious commodities, for example, legitimate art). And in a structurally similar way to the logic of the field of production, it is more effective to produce difference through qualitative than quantitative consumption. One Bentley amounts to a higher sign value than four Toyotas. An important difference between exchange and sign value, then, would be that sign value cannot be accumulated in the same way as economic exchange value. The symbolic value of the sign does not have the additive quality of economic value; It is not a quantity but rather a quality. However, to the opposite of this, Bourdieu argues that different forms of capital indeed *can* be converted through the exchange of commensurable objects:

> The universal equivalent, the measure of all equivalences, is nothing other than labor-time (in the widest sense); and the conservation of social energy through all its conversions is verified if, in each case, one takes into account both the labor-time needed to transform it from one type to another. (Bourdieu 1983/1986: 253)

We shall return to labour and its role in the fields of culture and media production and consumption in a subsequent chapter, and also to the problem of convertibility.

***

In this chapter I have tried to account for the perspective and analytical model that I will put to work in subsequent chapters. I want to emphasise that in some chapters this is indeed a question of perspective. The next chapter, for example, will deal mainly with the premises and characteristics of media and cultural production in the contemporary media environment. In the following chapter on labour, I will more fully activate this analytical model to discuss media use in terms of both production and consumption.

Chapter 3
New Organisational Forms of Value Production

A key component that affects the ways value is created in media production and consumption is the organisational forms of production – how media companies through various techniques such as tight diversification or horizontal integration seek to control content and the distribution of media content across technological platforms (as media content obviously appear across platforms from TV-web-mobile phones, or records-radio-iPods-mobile phones, etc). This integration most often involves traditional mass media in connection with the web and mobile phones. Much of this has to do with changes in the business models of the media (in which 'old' models from the mass media are combined with technological solutions provided by, for example, the web). An important factor in these business models is the relation to the media users, and the ways these are regarded from the perspective of producing institutions. This chapter will discuss some of the new business models that are adopted or tried out. These will be contrasted with older business models, and an analysis will be done on the relationship between the new and the old business models.

In the early 1990s, in the wake of the rise of digital media, the Internet and the World Wide Web and their increased abilities for mediated interpersonal communication, the concepts of mass media, mass communication and mass audience became increasingly contested. This was perhaps phrased most drastically by the best-selling author of the science-fiction novel *Jurassic Park*, Michael Crichton, in an article in *Wired* in 1993, arguing that 'Today's mass media is tomorrow's fossil fuel' (quoted in Jensen, 1998: 39). To Crichton, the mass media were nothing but the 'mediasaurus', doomed to extinction because of their clumsiness and inability to adjust to changed environmental conditions.

As a replacement for the mass concepts, new terms such as new media, or indeed personal media, came to be suggested. These concepts, naturally, are not only meant to replace the old mass concepts. They also forefront varied characteristics of the supposedly new. The concept of 'new media', then, became a catch phrase for digital, computer-based communication technologies (see, for example, Wardrip-Fruin and Montfort 2003; for criticism, see Drotner 2002, Lagerkvist 2009). The concept of personal media instead forefronts the medium's functional relation to its users and its privileging of interpersonal communication via e-mail, chat and instant messaging (Lüders 2008). Arguably, interpersonal, real-time communication at a distance has existed a long time via the telephone (although the telephone also had its 'mass moment' in its early experimental phase, with mass broadcasts of, that is, concerts [see Marvin 1988/1995]), but today these media are also mobile, and follow the user wherever he or she goes.

The technological reason for decoupling the prefix 'mass' from 'communication' and 'media' was paralleled by developments in media research. A first point of criticism of the mass concept was, of course, Raymond Williams's (1958/1963: 300) conclusion that 'there are in fact no masses, there are only ways of seeing people as masses'. Since then this point has been central to media research, and naïve uses of the mass concept have accordingly been sparse. As audience research, especially reception theory, subsequently pointed to the fact that even similar messages or works were interpreted in very different ways depending on a range of social, cultural and contextual factors (for example, Morley 1986, Liebes and Katz 1990/1993), the mass message was further deconstructed, and what was left were variations of interpretations. With the further development of reception theory into 'media ethnography' (see Drotner 1993, Bolin 1994a) and the 'third phase' of audience research (Alasuutari 1999), this also led to the decentring of the media: Whereas reception theory had concentrated on the relationship between an interpreting subject and a work – or 'meaningful discourse', as Stuart Hall (1973) put it – the focus now became fixed to the interpreting subject and the context of the media content. The ethnographic turn in audience studies thus became the ultimate kiss of death for the concept of the mass audience.

The distinctions made between the 'old' mass media and the 'new' digital media have mainly concerned the functional aspects of the technologies, that is, the ways users can adopt and engage in the many interactive functions of the digital media. However, although early Internet ideology held that 'information wants to be free', today this freedom is sharply circumscribed by commercial interests. The commercialisation of the web has, of course, met with substantial debate and criticism. However, few debaters have analysed the organisational forms of this specific commercialisation process and compared or related the business models of the old mass media to the new business models of the digital, personal media.

In this chapter I will try – from a historical perspective – to fill this space by discussing similarities and differences between 'old' mass media business models and new digital network models, in which 'behavioural targeting', 'asynchronous ads', contextual targeting' and 'advergaming' are becoming the tools for capturing the 'digital consumer'.

I will firstly say something about traditional mass communication, mass media and the mass audience, and list some of their characteristics as commonly described in the literature. I will then do the same with the new, digital, personal media, and distinguish them from their mass counterparts (but also point to some weaknesses in the accounts given of the differences). In the third section, I will briefly discuss the characteristics of traditional business models of the media (personal as well as mass media). In the fourth section I will then give some examples of how these traditional models have changed, and how some new techniques and approaches have appeared. Fifthly, I will describe some of the features of new, digital business models, formed around the personal media, and also take advantage of them as just personal media. In the concluding section I will then summarise what is new and what is not, in my analysis of the historical changes that have led up to today's media business models. My general argument is that we should acknowledge the similarities between the business models connected to the old mass media and the new, digital media, as this helps us better understand how they work.

I will discuss this partly as an oscillation between a phenomenological media user perspective, or perhaps a social perspective if you will, and an industry or business perspective. One of my points is that we have seen too little of this dual perspectivation, and that this fact also explains why debaters firmly grounded in the social perspective of media users and reception studies do not make full accounts for the forms of domination and asymmetrical communication that are the dialectical opposite of the perceived symmetric communication connected to the user possibilities of the personal media.

The basic argument is, then, that the perceived freedom of choice and creativity that the individual media user can experience is also at the root of the new digital business models in which this freedom is converted into economic value within the media industries.

Masses, Mass Media and Mass Communication

It can be argued that 'mass theory' arrived around the turn of the century 1900 with writers such as Gustav le Bon and José Ortega y Gasset publishing their accounts of the effects of modernisation and industrialisation. Le Bon's (1896/2006) *The Crowd: A Study of the Popular Mind* was a very early account of mass or group psychology, in which he argues that the individual loses some of his critical abilities and becomes the subject of easy manipulation when caught up in the crowd. It should be noted that le Bon never used the concept of mass. The original French title was *La psychologie des foules*, which also highlights its psychological perspective (the early Swedish translation from 1912, however, used the mass concept: *Massans psykologi*). A few decades after le Bon's publication, writing in the period between the two world wars, Spanish philosopher José Ortega y Gasset (1930/1964) published *The Revolt of the Masses*, which also focussed on the psychology of mass man in a similar vein as le Bon. To Ortega y Gasset, the mass was a quality bound to the individual, a state of mind (or, perhaps, absence of mind):

> Strictly speaking, the mass, as a psychological fact, can be defined without waiting for individuals to appear in mass formation. In the presence of one individual we can decide whether he is 'mass' or not. The mass is all that which sets no value on itself – good or ill – based on specific grounds, but which feels itself 'just like everybody,' and nevertheless is not concerned about it; is, in fact, quite happy to feel itself as one with everybody else. (Ortega y Gasset, 1930/1964: 14f)

Around the same time, German writer Siegfried Kracauer also used the mass concept in 'The Mass Ornament' (1927/1995) in an attempt at understanding Weimar culture, and in so doing presented a far more positive, even celebratory, account of various phenomena connected to mass and popular culture.

Shortly after the Second World War the mass debate arose again, engaging writers such as Edward Shils (1961), Paul Lazarsfeld (1961), Bernard Rosenberg and David Manning White (1957), and others. This discussion is partly still occupied with the psychological character of the individual, as in David Riesman's (1950/1955) famous *The Lonely Crowd*, but a new and strong feature in the discussion is the impact of modern broadcast mass media, most notably television. Since television developed earlier in the US than it did in Europe or any other part of the world, it comes as no surprise that those engaged in this debate were foremost US researchers and cultural critics, or in some cases, European immigrants living in the US.

This is then the moment at which media theory started to engage in the mass debate, and when the concepts of mass communication, mass media and mass audiences started to be defined. One such common definition of the mass communication and media was provided by sociologist Charles Wright (1959) in his aptly titled book *Mass Communication*. Here he defined 'the nature and functions of mass communication' along three main characteristics: the nature of the audience, the nature of the communication experience, and the nature of the communicator. According to Wright, the mass communicated audience should be 'large, heterogeneous, and anonymous' (p. 13). The nature of the communication experience should be characterised as 'public, rapid, and transient' (p. 14), and the communicator was supposed 'to be, or operate within, a complex organization that may involve great expense' (p. 15).

Indeed, this definition changed very little over the years until the mid-1990s, which can be seen in, for example, John Thompson's (1995) characteristics in *The Media and Modernity*, in which he distinguishes between different forms of social interaction as 'face-to-face', 'mediated', and 'mediated quasi-interaction', whereby the third is characterised by 'separations of contexts' and 'extended availability in time and space', 'narrowing of the range of symbolic cues', 'oriented towards an indefinite range of potential recipients', and ultimately 'monological' (p. 85). Mediated quasi-interaction obviously shares many features with Wright's mass communication, and there are naturally many others who with smaller variations have tried to pin down this specific type of communication (see, for example, Luhmann, 2000).

And what characterises mass communication naturally also characterises the media through which this specific kind of communication is carried out.

Mass communication and mass media also produced the mass audience. In Denis McQuail's (1997) words, the mass audience:

> was itself a product of several forces: urban concentration; technologies
> of relatively cheap dissemination (economies of scale); limited supplies of

'software' (media content) and high costs of individual reception; social centralization (monopolism or statism); and nationalism. (McQuail 1997: 128)

However, McQuail also holds that the concept of audience today is increasingly contested as a meaningful category. Indeed, he puts forth the question of whether we have witnessed 'the end of the audience?' (McQuail 1997: 127), and as Vincent Mosco and Lewis Kaye (2000: 45) have pointed out, the concept of audience was at any rate born in executive rooms of 'the marketing departments of companies with a stake in selling products through the media'. This fact led John Ellis (1992) to conclude that it might then be wise to distinguish between the marketing concept of audience as a statistical aggregate, and viewers, readers and listeners as the social subjects interpreting and using the media.

Personal Media and Communication Modes

To the contrary of the de-individualised mass media and communication model, during the past decade alternatives have been put forward that argue that the media do not have such uniform influence over users, and that new, digital media should rather be considered 'personal media' (Lüders et al. 2007, Lüders 2008). A common train of thought is that 'during the past ten to fifteen years a range of new media have appeared, in front of which we cannot put the prefix "mass"' (Rasmussen 2007: 259; my translation).

Marika Lüders defines personal media as:

> the tools for interpersonal communication and personalized expression, for example, mobile phones, email, Instant Messenger, homepages, private weblogs (blogs), online profiles and photo-sharing sites. (Lüders 2008: 684)

She also names a few characteristics of these personal media, whereby '[p] rivate individuals create personal media content in non-institutionalized settings' (p. 693), and where 'the most distinguishable feature of personal media, barring a few exceptions, is the required type of activity of all parts involved as actors in more or less symmetrical communication processes' (p. 685).

These arguments are also put forth by Australian researchers such as Axel Bruns (2008) and John Banks and Sal Humphreys (2008), who emphasise the symmetry and cooperative efforts of users, or 'produsers', engaging in 'produsage' (in Bruns' terms).

Personal media, then, supposedly offer more freedom to their users, privileging interpersonal communication and simplifying processes of production so that everyone becomes a potential media producer. However, we should perhaps be cautious of overstating the freedom of users, since the degrees to which they act in 'non-institutionalized settings' can vary substantially. Arguably, a profile page on Facebook or any other social networking site might be complex in its construction, artistic elements, etc., but Facebook is hardly a non-institutionalised setting – it is quite the contrary, as will be further discussed below. This is not denying that non-institutionalised communication occurs through digital media. Of course it does. But this is hardly a new feature, since amateur fan media production, as well as amateur family filming, existed long before the rise of digital media (see Bolin 1998). Admittedly, digital media has increased the opportunities for amateur or non-institutionalised production, but it is important not to forget the pre-forms of this type of production. Indeed, the interpersonal communication component of personal media did not arrive with digital media, as telephones and letters have also existed a long time.

'Old' Broadcast Business Models

Traditionally, the mass media have been organised around two basic economic business models, centred around two basic commodities: texts and audiences (cf. Bolin 2009). The text-based model builds on selling copies of texts and first appeared in print media with early publishing houses, and then with newspapers. The audience-based model, which builds on the principle of selling audiences to advertisers, appeared for the first time in newspapers. Newspapers then eventually came to combine the text-based and the audience-based models (that is, selling copies of newspapers to readers and then selling the same readers as statistically comprised in groups to advertisers), but generally one could say that the text-based model precedes the audience-based model (Gustafsson 2009).

Historically, the *text-based model* was developed during early industrialisation and mass production of the written word, at a time when the written word came to be commodified.[1] The customer received a printed copy, and the seller was economically compensated in return. The author, distributor and seller could naturally not know who or how many actually read the books or printed commodities. However, they knew how many copies they had sold, which is also the basic and fundamental idea behind the model. In fact, from an economic perspective, it is irrelevant how many readers a book has, as its economic success is counted in terms of how many copies are sold. Over the years the text-based model has become slightly differentiated; Whereas you once paid per bought copy, you can today also subscribe or pay licence fees. The basic feature, however, is that as long as things sell, no-one wonders very much who or how many actually use the text.

Just like the text-based model, the *audience-based model* was first developed within print media, or more exactly within the printed press. In 1914, advertisers in the US established the Audit Bureau of Circulation to verify readership (Beniger 1986, quoted in Webster and Phalen 1997: 5). The audience-based model was then

---

1   Early forms of commercial publishing houses could be found in ancient Rome (Nordenstreng 1977: 27), but it is probably fair to say that it is first during industrialisation that the commodification of the printed word takes its full form.

further adopted within the radio industry in the US in the 1920s (Webster and Phalen 1997: 3; Barnouw 1978/1979: 16ff). Radio programmes were initially produced as a means for selling transmitters, and it was only after several years that sponsors entered the stage, producing full-length programmes (initially only the title gave away who the sponsor was). This system was transferred to television with the arrival of this new medium, but when production costs increased in the 1950s the system changed from the sponsoring of programmes to the buying of slots for commercials during and between programmes (Barnouw 1978/1979: 58).

The basic difference between the two models is, then, that the text-based model builds on sold copies and the producer does not need to know more than how many copies are sold, whereas the audience-based model builds on how many supposedly read or engage with the programme texts, or, more precisely, the advertisements that surround them. And this calls for the development of methods to determine who actually comes into contact with the ads. Accordingly, increasingly new methods for trying to come to grips with who is actually watching, reading or listening have been developed.

Everyone knows that measuring audiences is difficult, and that methodologically there is a range of insecurities when it comes to the interpretation of audience figures (Ang 1991). However, as Thomas Streeter (1996: 281) points out, the 'most striking fact about the statistically mediocre character of ratings is how little industry members care about it'. So, irrespective of the uncertainties of audience measurement, both broadcasters and advertisers know that unless everyone acts *as if* the statistics are hard facts, the system will break down altogether (for a fuller discussion of this, see Bolin 2009).

Before we move on to discuss the updates of the business models, it might be appropriate to remind ourselves of a third model, born not from the mass media but from what could be called the early forms of personal media: the telephone and the letter. These are media, or perhaps rather organisational forms of communication, that unlike the mass media do not have any specific content. The communication's organisation provides the infrastructure, and the content of the communication is provided by its users. In this respect the telephone and the mail are more like services provided by communication organisations. What users pay for is the ability to use a communication network to communicate with distant others. We buy a stamp in order to be able to use the postal system, and we pay a rate (and perhaps also a fee per call we make) for the privilege of using the phone. We might call this third model the *service-based business model*. Arguably, the new business models of digital media can be considered a mix of the forms of mass communication and interpersonal communication like the phone and the mail service.

Updates of the Old Business Models

Initially, the audience-based model privileged a drive towards audience maximisation – the larger the audience, the better. At the turn of the 21st century, audience maximisation became ineffective within broadcasting as well as in the periodical press, and due to competition in the marketing industry, it was no longer the largest possible audience that was sought after but rather the *right* audience within a well-defined target group. These changes – partly driven by 'traditional' rationalisations within the capitalist system and partly as responses to national legislation and regulation – led to adjustments to the business models among the various parts of the media industries. Within the press, most notably the weeklies and monthlies, increasingly more targeted products were presented (and the magazines that attracted broader readerships were correspondingly abandoned). One could therefore see a plethora of niche magazines addressed to well-defined consumer groups: for example, the Swedish quarterly magazine *Rosie* (Bonniers), launched in April 2007 and targeting an audience of women with small gardens and balconies. However, this audience segment proved even too narrow for advertisers, and *Rosie* published its last issue towards the end of 2008.[2] However, although this particular magazine did not meet with commercial success, it reveals a way of thinking in the magazine business whereby content is tailored on the grounds of audience segmentation.

The broadcast media also increasingly developed towards niche audiences, as characterised by traditional sociological variables of age, sex, income and education, etc. Adding to this was lifestyle segmentation techniques, such as Nielsen's 'Minerva lifestyle segmentation'. Minerva, and similar analyses such as Orvesto, focusses on patterns of consumption among viewers, whereby the consumption of certain lifestyle commodities is correlated to the consumption of other commodities and services (see Bolin 2002: 195). Today, niche thinking has led broadcasters to differentiate their content to several platforms of distribution. This means that TV4, since 1991 the main commercial broadcaster in Sweden, for example, is not one television channel, but 'around 30' (as of December 2010): TV4, TV4 Sport, TV4 Film, TV4 Science Fiction, etc. All these channels are addressed to specific audience segments to meet demands from advertisers, and although audience statistics show a steady decrease for the main channel TV4, the total audience for all the media house's channels have increased.

To niche audiences along sociological variables is, however, but one way of rationalising audience production. Another example of how advertising strategies become more refined within broadcast television can be taken from TV4 as well, until recently bound to certain public service obligations through its licence agreements with the Swedish state.[3] One of the obligations TV4 had to live up to

---

2   Personal communication with Lena Thelenius, marketing manager at Bonnier Tidskrifter, 13 September 2009.

3   With the full digitisation of the Swedish broadcasting system, today TV4 is no longer bound to this agreement, which it entered into in exchange for being the only national commercial channel, reaching all parts of the Swedish population. With the advent of digitisation TV4's main commercial competitors, TV3 and Kanal 5, also have the same reach.

for its first 15 years in operation was to produce and direct programmes for *all* of Sweden, that is, not only to the urban middle classes but also to the rural areas, which are quite numerous in Sweden.

However, as a commercial broadcaster TV4 has had to adjust to which audiences are in demand among advertisers. And there are certain groups that are in less demand than others: older, retired people, for example. This means that it is not only general ratings that are crucial, but more specifically *target rating points* (TRP). For TV4 the target group is the 12-59 year age group, which means that of Sweden's 9 million inhabitants 5.7 million belong to the target group. In economic terms all other viewer groups, comprising around 3.3 million Swedes, are worthless; That is, they cannot be sold on the market for audiences. As audiences, then, these groups are merely a by-product of the system, and the broadcaster will concentrate on the core target audience.

It is very easy to see how TV4 has struggled with this contradiction between advertiser demand and the obligations written into their licence agreement with the state. In the early 1990s, the main advertising strategy was 'specific', which means that advertisers buy advertising time in connection to a specific programme. Advertising rates naturally vary – it is of course more expensive to advertise during prime time, for example – and are based on estimates of how many viewers a certain programme attracts. However, for TV4 as a national broadcaster, prices for prime-time commercials soon become quite high, and only the most economically strong companies tend to advertise. In order to broaden the advertising base TV4 introduced DIRR, a Swedish abbreviation for 'Differentierad regional reklam', which roughly translates into 'Differentiated Regional Advertising'. Initially, the long-stretched geographic area of Sweden was divided into 16 regions (today 30), where they had local news production as well as some local programming broadcast during 'windows' in the ordinary schedule. This meant that as they attracted local audiences they could also regionally differentiate the commercials, and hence smaller, local business enterprises could afford to advertise. Today, this local commercial revenue makes up more than 20 per cent of the broadcasting company's turnover (circa 600 million SEK [2010], or approximately 60 million EUR).[4]

The main advantage of this is the ability to differentiate the regions into advertising units. Sweden is a country that stretches out for 1,574 kilometres from north to south. This means that there are many regional differences between the most southern and the most northern areas. Through a division of the nation into regions, all regions can be separated and individually targeted with advertisements. This refinement of the channel's advertising strategies has a number of consequences. Firstly, it makes it possible for advertisers who would

---

4 Figures for 2010 are estimates based on advertising sales, which had already reached 600 million SEK at the beginning of December 2010, according to Åsa Severed, CEO of the local channels of TV4 in an interview (*Medievärlden* 9 December 2010; www.medievarlden.se/nyheter/2010/12/tv4-sverige-tar-andelar-och-borjar-salja-play [Last accessed 9 December 2010].

never have been able to afford to broadcast on national television (since their potential customers are found only locally or regionally) to take advantage of the commercial possibilities of television. Secondly, it makes it possible to regionally adjust advertisements with national potential in time to suit regional markets. Since Sweden's outstretched geographical character means that winter arrives several months earlier in the north than it does far south, a commercial clip for, say, winter tires can be aired in October in the most northern parts, when it is still a couple of months until winter tires can – and according to Swedish legislation are allowed to – be used in the far south. From this follows that the audience commodity is not only structured by age, ethnicity, gender, educational level or settlement (large city, town, village, countryside), but also by *which* city, town, village or part of the countryside the audience segment can be found.

Another market strategy, introduced in 1998, is Run-By-Station (RBS). This means that the advertiser buys a certain number of 'contacts' in the target group, for example, a specific number of young, 20-year-old women living in large cities. TV4 then places the commercial close to, most often before, a television show (film, news broadcast, entertainment show) that attracts this very segment. And when the commercial has reached the audience size agreed upon with the advertiser, the deal is closed. In order to be cost-effective, TV4 obviously places the commercials as close as possible to those shows that attract the 'right' audience, in order to maximise audience reach with as few transmissions as possible of every commercial clip. This naturally sets new demands for sophisticated instruments that can measure the audience for every single commercial, and accordingly, increasingly more effective ways of controlling the audience commodity this way have been developed. If the broadcaster is effective, it can reach the audience segments in few screenings and thus take on more advertisements, for other commodities that advertisers want to promote, and in the end produce more surplus value for their shareholders. This strategy can be viewed against the fact that the time for commercials TV4 has at its disposal has been restricted over the years by its license agreement with the state. The agreement initially contained two important restrictions. Firstly, until 2002 TV4 could not interrupt programmes with commercials. This is, of course, why shorter programmes were privileged by the channel over lengthier ones, and a reason why it has also tended to produce programmes in segments (such as the three parts of *Bingolotto*, cf. Bolin 2002). Secondly, there has always been a limit on how many commercials per hour and day TV4 can broadcast. One way to rationalise within the limits of these restrictions and regulations has been to develop more effective ways to use the time at their disposal, hence DIRR and RBS.

Regionalisation has thus proven economically successful for commercial TV4, and the revenues for local advertising are increasing. Commercial radio in Sweden did not have to regionalise, since the construction prescribed a regional structure already from the start. When commercial radio was introduced, it was in the form of local radio. As soon as the system was established, however, cartels bought local stations, and today the Swedish commercial radio landscape is nationally dominated by two companies that each run several stations: the Modern Times Group (MTG) and the Scandinavian Broadcasting System (SBS) (Forsman 2010: 207ff). These are administrated from Stockholm, where the major parts of the content are produced, but with local 'windows' in the form of locally produced content, thereby fulfilling the obligations set up in the concessions charters.

These are descriptions of national Swedish media conditions. Some markets, such as the one in which the music business is active, are highly transnational, dominated by a few large media conglomerates – in the case of the music business, by the 'big four': Universal, EMI, Warner and Sony/BMG (Burkart and McCourt 2006).

In conclusion, then, there are variations in the business models, depending on which media form you look at. The music business differs from the film industry, the press, television and radio, the computer game industry, the web, etc. In the late 1970s and early 1980s, however, many of these media productions sectors merged into media conglomerates (Burkart and McCourt 2006: 28), which Eric Rothenbuhler and John Dimick (1982) termed 'tight diversification'. According to Rothenbuhler and Dimick, a 'tightly diversified entertainment conglomerate is one that includes horizontally and vertically integrated firms from a range of media, including film, television, music and publishing' (quoted in Burkart and McCourt 2006: 28). In Sweden, both Bonniers and MTG can be considered tightly diversified corporations.

As Simon Frith (1988, quoted in Burkart and McCourt 2006: 23) has shown, secondary rights also became more important than primary rights around 1980, which means that it has become more profitable to do business with licences and copyright fees than to produce and sell your own records. The profits for the music business are said to be becoming increasingly comprised of licensing for music services, and today it is estimated that the big music corporations will earn up to 50 per cent of their revenues from music providers like Spotify within the upcoming five years. In 2009 Universal, for example, estimates that their income from music services will be around 20 per cent (SR P3 Nyheter 090722, 9.00).[5] Business models have thus changed from having been primarily centred on selling hard copies of vinyl and CDs to selling licenses and music services, whereby it is not the hard copy that is transferred between the seller and the customer but rather the right to experience the song online. Record companies have thus become what Burkart and McCourt (2006: 12) call music-service providers (MSP). This means that they are more engaged in selling the audiences for such services to advertisers than in selling content – this is thus a variation of the audience-based model.

---

5   Available online at: www.sr.se/p3. See also 'Digital Beethoven ger klirr i kassan', *Dagens Nyheter* 19 July 2009.

New Digital Business and Marketing Models

While the audience-based economic model – originally developed within the press and then further developed within the broadcast media – has been refined over the years, and niche audiences have become more important than mass audiences in the continuous strive for the most 'pure' audience commodity, web-based media are struggling hard to develop techniques that can be profitable for web producers. An early form of web advertising was banners, whereby advertisers put up small brand messages on specific websites that they thought were attractive to their audiences. Since the Internet audience is diffused and hard to track, advertising on the web has grown at a slower pace than expected. And although there is a great deal of insecurity over the audience figures for television, the degree of insecurity is even higher when it comes to measuring the web.

Nonetheless, a range of new techniques has been introduced, some of which have their early forms outside the web, and some of which have not. Astroturfing, for example, the technique of having a political, commercial or promotional campaign look as if it were a grassroots initiative, is one such technique that precedes the Internet. The use of shills is a similar technique, as is viral marketing, that is, the technique of using pre-existing social networks to enhance brand awareness or to promote specific consumer products. Viral marketing can take many forms, including 'advergaming', that is, having a computer game centred on a specific commodity. All these techniques precede the Internet, although the Internet has made them more easily orchestrated.

With the rise of the web, a range of new techniques has appeared for measuring audiences, or, rather, for measuring audience behaviour. When it comes to such techniques that have developed on the net, and indeed, build on the algorithms that can only be created on the net, these build on movement rather than on sociological variables. In the words of Elizabeth van Couvering (2008), the industry has developed the 'traffic commodity'.

In their analysis of the music industry, Burkhart and McCourt (2006) have pointed to its two main technologies: customer-relationship management (CRM) and digital-rights management (DRM). *Customer-relationship management* is the net-based equivalent to the Nielsen ratings system of the mass media, through which user behaviour is analysed. The knowledge gained from this analysis is then used to personalise the offers to the individual music listener/customer. The technology is not only used by the music industry but also by, for example, Internet bookstores such as Amazon, where you get tips on titles that might interest you based on your previous purchases. *Digital-rights management* is about control over content and aims at regulating online activities, and has a technical and a judicial side to it. Technologically it seeks to ensure that only paying customers get access to content, and that content is 'locked up' so that further copying or distribution is disabled. Judicially, it concerns hunting down and prosecuting those who infringe on copyrighted material. The internationally renowned Swedish court case against the file sharing site The Pirate Bay or, rather, the people responsible for the site, is a well-known example, but there are also many international cases in which large media corporations are suing individual file sharers.[6]

Digital-rights management, then, builds on the text-based business model, while customer-relationship management is more similar to the audience-based model, with the significant difference that what is traded is not the statistical aggregate of an audience that consumes texts in a given medium but rather the active audience communicating, searching or behaving on the net. Examples of customer-relationship management are *contextual* and *behavioural targeting*, or predictive behavioural targeting, as the latter technique is at times called in order to emphasise the future-oriented quality of improved profitability.

There are several agencies that specialise in contextual and behavioural targeting, such as nugg.ad in Germany, Phorm in the UK, and Adaptlogic in Sweden, who work under the slogan 'We deliver more valuable clicks'. Contextual targeting has been described by Joseph Turow (2006: 90) as the 'database marketing' technique whereby 'search engine firms make agreements with websites that allow their software to read the pages of the sites and places ads at the side of their web pages when they find words their advertising clients have chosen'.

Contextual targeting occurs, for example, when you buy a book from Amazon and then get an offer about buying another title, based on the fact that people who have bought the same book have also purchased other titles within the same genre. As I am writing this, I am listening to Spotify on the 'free' advertising-based version. I have searched and found a collection of music by Swedish opera tenor Jussi Björling, mainly because I find his version of 'Ack, Värmeland du sköna' such a great performance. I am not an opera aficionado – in fact I rarely listen to this kind of music – and because of this I cannot help noticing that all the commercials that interrupt my listening are for other opera music, which I care very little for and mostly do not recognise at all. These are not the commercials I am used to, and of course this is a case of my being contextually targeted. I only happen to notice this because I have chosen a genre I generally do not listen to. These are the moments when contextual targeting fails, when we at times depart from our ordinary habits, when we think of ourselves as genuinely individual – and are immediately reminded of our more repetitive, habitual and highly predictable selves.

Contextual and behavioural targeting is presented by advertising agencies to users in positive terms as a way of exchanging 'irrelevant information' and spam with 'useful' information. With this move, the advertising business comes close to the rhetoric of advertising as consumer information. As Turow has shown based on attitudes among US consumers, personalised targeted messages, in combination with market discrimination based on consumer performance (the more you spend

---

6 Other examples include 'Åtalad yngling slår tillbaka mot skivindustrin', *Dagens Nyheter*, 29 July 2009. Available at http://www.dn.se/kultur-noje/nyheter/atalad-yngling-slar-tillbaka-mot-musikindustrin-1.920559 [Last accessed 10 August 2009]. See also Andersson and Snickars (2010) for thorough discussions on the Pirate Bay court case.

and the more loyal you are as a consumer to a certain brand, the better deals you are offered), provoke competition between consumers, who come to envy others who they feel have received better offers – presumably because they have performed 'better' and are thus more highly valued by the retail business (Turow 2006).

The technology of database marketing and the tailoring of individualised and contextualised commercial messages build on the collection of large amounts of data. It is only with these large aggregates of consumer information that it is possible to effectively target small groups of consumers and even individuals with personalised messages. As Hugo Drayton, CEO of British 'innovative digital technology company' Phorm, states: 'With access to ISP data, we have an enormous bowl to fish'.[7] With our lives being increasingly played out on the web, this bowl is indeed growing.

On the web pages of German agency nugg.ad (http://www.nugg.ad), the address is seemingly ambivalent: With the caption 'Predictive Behavioural Targeting ... keeps her in style', a young woman smiles happily at the viewer, holding a shopping bag tight to her chest, thus indicating a service to ordinary consumers. Ordinary shoppers, however, are hardly the main target of these messages. The promotional material is rather directed at potential customers of nugg.ad, that is, 'advertisers', 'publishers' and 'adnetworks'. The rhetoric of the 'satisfied consumer' possibly aims at convincing those consumers who accidentally find their way to nugg.ad's web pages that it is in their interest that the techniques have been developed.

The advertising business is, quite naturally, highly aware of the ethical issues surrounding these kinds of marketing models, and knows that if consumers become suspicious of their surveillance techniques, campaigns can easily backfire. Hence the will to present this as a form of help to the consumer, or to point to consumer power: 'Audiences now have the same power as elite media organisations' was a statement made by communications consultant Ian Leslie at the Changing Advertising Summit 2008 in London (13 October, 2008), an annual event arranged by the British newspaper *The Guardian* (MediaGuardian) since 2007, where advertisers, search engine companies, promoters, web optimisers and other interested parties in such kinds of businesses gather to discuss the future of advertising and to share their respective technical and economic models. We can thus see that the rhetoric behind the academic analysis of personal media that, for example, Lüders and others engage in (for example, Lüders 2008) and the rhetoric of the industry at times overlap.

The business models around these techniques have begun to involve co-operations between advertising networks, Internet service providers and search engines. The British company Phorm has developed such an intermediate service that connects all these actors in the field, to the presumed economic benefit of all. This is done through their platform OIX, which stands for Open Internet

---

7   Quoted from Drayton's keynote speech at the Changing Advertising Summit 2008, London 13 October.

Exchange. On its web pages Phorm states that 'The OIX replaces irrelevant ads with what's interesting for you'.[8]

The 'you' addressed by the promotional material is ambiguous, possibly intentionally. To the consumer, it reads as if he or she will get the right information about consumer products, and to the commercial actor it indicates possible economic benefits. The new web pages of OIX more specifically address the corporate customers:

> The Open Internet Exchange (OIX) is revolutionising the online advertising industry. Its innovative platform and key partnerships — with advertisers, agencies, publishers and ad networks and ISPs — create value and opportunity throughout the digital advertising ecosystem. The OIX is powered by Phorm's proprietary ad serving technology, which uses anonymised ISP data to serve the right ad to the right user at the right time — the right number of times. (www. oix.com/index.html, last accessed 9 August 2009)

The dual address to consumers as well as business partners is also found in several places in Phorm's promotion material, where what they call the 'privacy revolution' is supposedly to function as a comfort to consumers, enhanced by the promise 'benefits to all' – a classic 'win-win' rhetoric common in the advertising business.

Extended Commodification of the Lifeworld – The Smartphone

Contextual and behavioural targeting are database marketing techniques that would not have been possible to develop without digitisation and mass data mining. Digitisation is, as was already noted in the introduction, a key driver in the dual process of increased media user opportunities and the increased control and surveillance by the media industry of the same users. The media industry likes to think of this as the management of customer relations (customer-relationship management). However, this is hardly a symmetrical relationship, as the power to regulate this relationship resides one-sidedly with the media companies.

Database marketing naturally helps to commodify areas of our lifeworlds previously freed from the market. Whenever we switch on our computers at home and log into our favourite social network sites, employ search engines or surf the web seemingly at random, our very behaviour becomes subsumed by the market, and in minute digital detail we feed the system with information that is ultimately bought and sold on the market for Internet surveillance.

Capital, however, is continuously seeking new areas to subsume. If the personal computer provided such an opportunity for extension when it was disseminated in such magnitude that data mining techniques proved profitable, the mobile phone

---

8   www.phorm.com [Last accessed 20 April 2009].

has provided yet another such extension. At the moment (2010), the ITU reports that approximately 90 per cent of the world's population have access to mobile networks. Furthermore, of the 5.3 billion mobile subscriptions in the world, 940 million are for 3G services. This should be compared with the estimated figure of two billion Internet users by the end of 2010 (ITU 2010). As we move into 4G technology this will add to this development, as a faster broadband structure will make more features of mobiles more user-friendly.

As Gerard Goggin (2009: 235) has noted, the iPhone (and other smartphones, one might add), 'pushes the mobile much more towards the computers and the internet'. As a mobile user this naturally open for new communication possibilities, and surely few smartphone users would argue that the gadget has not changed mobile behaviour. With freedom comes its dialectical opposite, however, in new forms of surveillance. As Mark Andrejevic (2007) has argued, the increased use of digital equipment makes us vulnerable to new kinds of surveillance. As today's smartphone has all the possibilities of the computer, we can use it to surf the web, check our position on the GPS, check the weather forecast, answer the most urgent e-mails, listen to our favourite music on Spotify or whatever other music service we have, watch television and much more. All these activities leave their digital traces behind for data mining, storage and refinement into the 'traffic commodity' (van Couvering 2008).

Some have lamented the fact that mobile advertising has not taken off (for example, Wilken and Sinclair 2010). However, the smartphone does seem to develop its own business models, without remediating old advertising models from the computer. As the mobile has one competitive advantage over the computer – it is mobile – it can also take advantage of (or rather advertisers take advantage of) its geographical positioning tools, in order to produce not just the traffic commodity but the *mobile traffic commodity*. Advertisers have experienced a problem with mobile and flexible audiences, who promiscuously drift between television and radio channels, different print magazines, etc. With the mobile phone, however, mobility is turned from a problem into an asset.

Historically, the revenues from mobile phone technology have been based on traffic: sent and received voice calls and text messages. With the new functions of the smartphone (e-mail, social networking, web surfing), several new forms of this traffic commodity emerge. Not only do these new functions add increased amounts of new transferred megabytes, and thereby contribute to more general traffic; Some of the functions also provide information on behaviour and context, making the smartphone similar to the computer in being the basis for contextual and behavioural targeting. Its geographical positioning abilities also make it possible not only 'to serve the right ad to the right user at the right time — the right number of times', as Phorm promises its customers, but also to target this consumer in the *right place*.

Location-based advertising thus adds a new layer to the already existing technologies for capturing the digital consumer. And the more data that can be accessed, the larger the 'fish bowl', and the more efficient the consumer surveillance will be. Accordingly, search engines such as Yahoo or Google, with their vast amounts of data, have good possibilities to crawl consumers on the web. Thus the CEO of Google, Eric Schmidt, was quoted saying that if the company 'look at enough of your messaging and your location, and use artificial intelligence, we can predict where you are going to go'.[9]

These kinds of targeting practices are of course hard to mask for customers, as it will take little in terms of consideration to understand that the marketing offer you just received via SMS on buying a new flat-screen television set, while passing by a store with that exact set on display, was triggered by a sophisticated algorithm that took advantage of your geographic position. This is also why consent is, if not needed, then a wise strategy. At the shopping mall Skrapan in the inner city of Stockholm, Sweden, customers are offered membership in the customer club of the mall, with the promise of receiving 'exclusive offers, benefits and invitations via SMS direct in your mobile', on the condition that you agree to allow the club to 'localise my mobile's position in order to send special offers and invitations at the right time, at the right place' (my translation).

So, what was an image of the future in Mark Andrejevic's *iSpy* (2007) is today more common practice in public settings, thus equalling public space with commercial space in ways that were not possible just a decade ago. Andrejevic's main argument is that we are witnessing a 'digital enclosure' of unprecedented proportion, whereby new areas of public and private life are continuously being subsumed the market (that is, a digital version of the commodification thesis). With reference to Walter Benjamin's *Arcades Project* (Benjamin 1982/1999), Andrejevic draws an analogy between the Paris arcades of the 19th century, where the overarching structure of glass and steel served to enclose the street in a 'bourgeois interior', and the digital environment, where the 'smart landscape, populated with receptors for portable digital devices, conserves the promise of interiority ... subsuming all physical space to the imperatives of a virtual marketplace' (Andrejevic 2007: 118f).

However, one might argue that the digital enclosure described by Andrejevic is but one in a line of media technologies used to administer consumers in public and semi-public settings. Historically this goes back to the use of cinema – between 1896 and 1898, a department store in the Galleria Umberto I in Naples, Italy, sponsored public film screenings to attract customers (Bruno 1993: 38f). Television has always been used for such purposes, not to mention music, or Muzak (Sterne 1997). As I have discussed in relation to a study of a Swedish shopping mall that I was part of around the turn of the Millennium, and in which I specifically studied the use of television in public spaces, media are the soft structuring tools that together with the hard, physical environment, serve to make customers flow smoothly through consumer settings (Bolin 2004a). In interviews, the site manager

---

9   'No anonymity on future web says Google CEO', Thinq.co.uk, 5 August 2010. Available online at: http://www.thinq.co.uk/2010/8/5/no-anonymity-future-web-says-google-ceo/ [Last accessed 3 November 2010].

of the shopping mall had elaborate thoughts on how to create the perfect 'flow' of customers through the aisles, especially through specifically designed music, whereby he found 'soft Cuban rhythms' the most appropriate for this task. These soft structuring strategies were also combined with hard structuring adjustments, such as removing benches in the mall, in order not to have the flow of customers interrupted (p. 138).

'From Mass Marketing to Mass Personalisation'

To conclude this chapter I will list some of the new, as well as some of the not-so-new, features of these business models. Firstly, it is quite clear from my examples above that the Internet provides the media, culture and advertising business with a range of new technological possibilities in their search for the media audience and its members. All of this is of course new, although offline pre-forms of shills, astroturfing, advergaming and viral marketing techniques most often exist. We must, for example, not forget all the efforts made by Hollywood to build entire films on industrial messages: Think of the blockbuster *Top Gun* (1986), which was produced with the kind help of the US Navy (albeit after some alterations to the script), with the effect of dramatically increased recruitment figures by some 500 per cent (Robb 2004: 182). The web makes some of these techniques more intrusive, however, something that is obviously noted by the business.

However, it is equally clear that successful platforms for such business models (for example, Google, Facebook, etc.) are genuinely appreciated by their users, who willingly accept the offer to communicate within the framework of this commercial environment (at least as long as the commercials are not experienced as too intrusive). This appreciation will take many individual expressions, revealing in a varied range of individual behaviours.

Still, if we look beyond the individual technologies used, and the individual behaviours enacted, we need to recognise that the consumer addressed by the media industry is similar to that which the traditional, mass media industry tried – and still tries – to capture. The task has merely changed from trying to capitalise on mass media audiences to 'Monetising the social web'.[10] So, we can expect a continuous move away from the text-based business model of the media, as I referred to it above, towards a more intensified hunt for revenues from services and social networking sites, towards the audience-based model. However, this audience-based model is also mixed with characteristics from the service model that was – and still is – the basic model for the telephone and postal systems. The

---

10   Quoted from the title of the panel session 'Community communications and "me media": Monetising the social web', at the Changing Advertising Summit, London, 13 October 2008. Interestingly enough, participants in the panel included, besides marketers from companies such as Honda, Facebook, MySpace and Mydeco, a representative of the charity organisation Oxfam, who obviously also contributes to this rhetoric.

service model does not produce content but rather opportunities to communicate through its infrastructure, and is mixed with the audience-based model, in which content is provided to attract audiences, so that they can be packaged and sold to advertisers. In this respect, it is equally misleading to talk of the power of consumers or media users for the social web as it is to talk of the power of telephone callers or mail senders.

As I have tried to illustrate above, although the new digital media have many features and uses that the old media lacked, from the viewpoint of the industry, no matter how dispersed the audiences are, they are still prey for advertisers along much the same principles as they were in the 'old' days of the monological, traditional mass media. So there is seemingly no contradiction between the audience feeling that they can contribute with user-generated content and that they can pick and choose among a wealth of media content on search portals such as blinkx, Google, etc. The advertising industry, in conjunction with ISPs and search engines, is still trying its hardest to 'capture the digital consumer', in the words of Mitch Lazar, Managing Director of Yahoo (quoted at the Changing Advertising Summit in October 2008). Being an active user of Facebook or Myspace might be satisfying to the individual user, but in aggregation these individuals are still treated as masses by the industry.

As mentioned at the beginning of this chapter, Raymond Williams (1958/1963) set the agenda for a more nuanced analysis of media audiences by proclaiming that masses are always constructions made by someone about collective others. This has been the guiding light within media research since then, and the statement has been empirically qualified in qualitative audience research of various kinds. The media industry has, however, been more reluctant to abandon the concept and the view on media users that accompanies it. *The Little Book of Integrated Marketing* (2008), published as promotional material by the advertising agency Alterian, describes the present movements within the business as the 'move from mass marketing to mass personalisation'. In relation to Williams's message, we can clearly see that although media research may have abandoned the view on media users as masses, especially qualitative, culturally inspired audience research, the media industries still regard their users as masses, albeit personalised ones.

However, there are also some new features in this view on audiences, and on the commodity produced jointly by the ISPs, web optimisers and search engines. If the old mass audience was constructed along sociological variables such as age, gender, socio-economic status, etc., the new mass audience consists of aggregated behaviour. So, the social subjects (media users, consumers) might feel personalised, but the industry cares little about these personalities and more about their behaviour, irrespective of who might be behind certain behaviours. So, while from the media user's perspective this is perceived of as personalisation, it is actually rather a question of customisation from the industry's point of view.

In the first few lines of 'The Mass Ornament', Siegfried Kracauer gives an account of a view on history that is strikingly similar to Walter Benjamin's, when he writes that:

> The position that an epoch occupies in the historical process can be determined more strikingly from an analysis of its inconspicuous surface-level expressions than from that epoch's judgement about itself. [...] The surface-level expressions, however, by virtue of their unconscious nature, provide unmediated access to the fundamental substance of the state of things. Conversely, knowledge about this state of things depends on the interpretation of these surface-level expressions. (Kracauer 1927/1995: 75)

In line with this, one can consider the return of the mass concept in the media industries as constituting the third wave of mass thinking, and an historical moment that connects the present mass moment with the previous two. These are historical moments occupying similar positions in the historical process, to speak with Krakauer (or Benjamin). These moments share the common feature of being centred on a shift in production and technology.

The first mass was the one formed by industrialisation, urbanisation and mass social movements around the turn of the century 1900, cinematically captured by Charlie Chaplin in *Modern Times* (1936) and theorised by Gustave le Bon, Ortega y Gasset and others, who wanted to understand psychological shifts in mass behaviour. This was not yet the mass formed by the media (indeed, to le Bon, writing in 1896, the only mass media were the print media) and not yet the mass audience, although it did not take long before the two became connected in early effects research and theories of uniform influences, for example the ideas that led up to the Payne Fund Studies in the late 1920s (cf. Jowett et al. 1996).

The second mass moment, however, was clearly formed on the basis of the media. With the fast and widespread use of television, questions of uniformity in behaviour reappeared on the agenda, after having been repressed for several decades. This is also the era in which industrialised mass culture came to be debated, not only in the US but also in Europe and elsewhere. The mass media were more clearly forefronted here, as were more general trends of cultural imperialism, etc. Thus it also grew out of technological change, a social and cultural shift that would forever change the character of Western societies.

The third mass moment also is the child of technological change, and I have already indicated the overwhelming consequences of the radical shift towards digital reproduction technologies we are witnessing today. These shifts have their historical parallel in the shift towards mechanical reproduction of art and culture that Walter Benjamin (1936/1977) discussed in his 'artwork' essay. As such, these are points in time that are structurally similar in their break with previous praxis in art and culture, and at which media technology helps alter social and cultural practices. They are also indicative of the philosophical view on history fostered by Benjamin (and Kracauer), which also has its epistemological qualities in helping us understand the present changes within the media and culture industries.

***

This chapter has largely taken the vantage point of production, especially the organisation of production and the business models connected to this organisation. This has meant a focus on the ways the media and culture industries relate to the users of cultural objects and commodities, especially how the industries create their basic commodities, be it aggregated mass or customised and personalised audiences. The commodities of the industries are, naturally, tools for the creation of economic value, and hence, this value form has been privileged in this chapter. In the next chapter I will shift focus and depart from the perspective of users and the value forms connected to them. As we will see, there are other values that result from the engagement of media users, and these will be privileged next.

Chapter 4
New Roles for Media Users: The Work of Consumption

The previous chapter focussed on the various strategies adopted in digital media production, and how these strategies can be related to earlier business models historically. One of the main characteristics of these new business models is the ways audiences (and media users) are addressed and consumed – the role the user is given in the media production process. This chapter will shift focus and discuss media users not as objects of strategies and business models in which they are used as raw material in the valorisation process, but as social subjects who actively orient themselves in and take advantage of the means of consumption/production, and sometimes also contribute to the production of media content. In the process of this media use, other forms of value besides the economic are created.

As has repeatedly been pointed out above, it can easily be argued that there has occurred a shift in how culture is produced and reproduced. This shift can mainly be attributed the digitisation of the media. It has already been pointed out that this change can be paralleled with the shift Walter Benjamin (1936/1977) observed in his analysis of the consequences of mechanical reproduction of artworks and popular culture. If Benjamin lived at the historical rupture of *mechanical reproduction*, we can see that we are currently in the age of *digital reproduction*. We can date the start of this era to the moment at which personal computers became accessible in large scale to non-professional users, which means that for the most technologically advanced countries it occurred sometime in the 1990s. Although digital computers were naturally around earlier than this, it is first with widespread access among ordinary media users, coupled with broadband and Wi-Fi technology, that the full extent of this shift can be seen.

As we have entered the age of digital reproduction, ordinary media users have increasingly gained access to means of production (and consumption) in the form of cheap, accessible and easily operated personal computers. With these means of production, the construction of media content becomes more accessible to users. However, it should also be acknowledged that productivity among media users has always existed, although the means for such production have been different. In media research there has accordingly been a longstanding debate about the active and productive audience as well as its opposite, the passive object of the media industries. An important issue to add to this discussion is, however, *what kinds of productivity* media users are engaged in, to what extent, in which ways, and with what consequences for the individual media user as well as for the media industry. And, addressing the overarching theme of this analysis, the question is how active media users contribute to the creation of various forms of value in the process of production and consumption.

This chapter will discuss how audiences as commodities or raw material can be related to readers, viewers, listeners and media users as constructors of identities and social difference. It is argued that in order to understand the mechanisms of media engagement we need to understand the underlying forms of value produced by both the media and culture industries as well as individuals engaging in media use. This double focus entails regarding audiences/media users as involved in two kinds of production-consumptions circuits, although with different functions in each: [1] In the first production-consumption circuit, the media user activities produce social difference (identities, cultural meaning, etc.) as well as non-commercial objects (for example, fan writing, amateur music-making) within the framework of a field of consumption, the product of which is then [2] made the object of productive consumption as part of the activities of the media industry in a field of cultural production. In this chapter I argue for the relevance of conceptually analysing these as separate circuits, and that the fallacy of much recent argument about the productive audience has misrecognised this difference, and conflated the processes connected to them. One of the keys to understanding this fallacy, I will argue, entails the concepts of work and labour, as these concepts have migrated from the analysis of media production to media use and reception, especially within the frameworks of what is usually called 'active audience theory'.

In the next section I will give a short historical account of the rise of active audience theory. In a second section I will discuss the production of social difference within what Bourdieu (1979/1989) would call fields of consumption, or, in the words of Baudrillard, the sphere where the consumption of sign commodities produce social difference (or distinction, as Bourdieu would put it). In this section I will give some examples of this production of difference. Then in a third section, and against the background of the examples in the second section, I will discuss this in terms of the work of consumption as well as the work of production. Here I will reconnect with the first section on the active audience theory, to make some distinctions between the various ways the concept of work is used. In a fourth section I will relate the work of consumption to the second production-consumption circuit, in which the labour carried out by consumers in acts of distinctions and differences is consumed within the framework of the field of digital cultural production. In the course of this discussion I will argue that the shift from analogue to digital production and consumption alters the ways we can understand the integration of cultural consumption and production.

The Two Active Audiences

A longstanding debate in media studies concerns the status of viewers, readers and listeners in relation to the media institutions, the media content these institutions disseminate, and the ways media users respond to this content. The main question has centred on whether audiences are passive recipients of media texts, masses that are duped into conformity by the media industries, or if media users are indeed active, critical and creative. The first position is often ascribed to effects research within the mainstream of mass communication research, or critical theory in the wake of the Frankfurt School, for whom audiences were seemingly fed with pseudo-individualised fodder, which created a social cement by which they were kept in false consciousness.

This position was contested by what might be called the first wave of active audience theory, namely uses and gratifications research. Research within this tradition held that audiences were not dupes of the culture industry but rather active subjects who picked and chose from a plurality of media texts, according to their own wishes and needs (for example, Blumler 1979). The uses and gratifications perspective was inherently psychologically oriented in its view on the media user, who was seen as an individual with psychological needs of a cognitive or emotional character that he or she wanted to have satisfied. The activity the media user engaged in was the very activity of trying to find media content that could fulfil this need. If the need was relaxation one might turn to entertainment, and if one needed information, one accordingly turned to news.

Another wave of active audience theory can be said to have been born from within British cultural studies, in the wake of Raymond Williams's (1961/1965) work on the analysis of culture as a 'whole way of life', and Richard Hoggart's (1957/1958) work on working-class cultures in Britain. Following from this interest in 'our common life together', as Williams put it, was also an intensified focus on the media contents that the working classes enjoyed, and a will to literally take popular culture seriously. Quite a few subsequent studies concerned youth and youth cultural practices, since these practices were seen as signifying 'magical solutions' to societal crises, and as a way of playing out working-class 'resistance through rituals' (Hall and Jefferson 1976/1991). This interest in the cultural habits of the working class (and youth) was then extended to other marginalised and under-researched groups, and hence gender and ethnicity also became important analytical categories on the research agenda and the cultural expressions women and immigrants engaged in landed in focus (cf. McRobbie 1980, Gillespie 1995). The active audience paradigm launched by cultural studies differs from the active audience in uses and gratifications theory. While in uses and gratifications research the active media user was a psychological individual acting based on his or her personal needs, the active audience member in cultural studies is a social being, analysed against class, age, gender or ethnicity. This is thus a more sociologically than psychologically founded audience. For the purposes of the analysis of value, this sociological category is of higher relevance, and hence the psychological needs of individual media users will not be discussed to as great a degree in the following.

The perspectives launched from within cultural studies were, however, also criticised by political economists, who argued that the focus on marginalised media users, and the meaning constructed by these marginalised groups, obscured the fact that although these media users might feel empowered by the contents they consumed and by acting out symbolic resistance, they were nonetheless dominated and in a subordinate position. The debate was sometimes quite fierce, exemplified in articles in the 1995 special issue of *Critical Studies of Mass Communication* where, for example, Nicholas Garnham (1995) accused representatives of the active audience perspective of bowing down in 'ethnographic worship' of media users, thus abandoning the critical position of research. Most fierce was perhaps William Seaman (1992), who a few years earlier had accused cultural studies scholars of engaging in 'pointless populism' (but see also the similar but more respectful debate between James Curran and David Morley in Curran et al. [1996]).

The debate has thus often been carried forward in polarising terms, with the opposing sides frequently reducing the other side's arguments. Admittedly, most effects studies have never had such grand claims as they are ascribed. Many are in fact quite aware of the limitations of their findings (see, for example, Eysenck and Nias 1978/1980: 77). Horkheimer and Adorno's arguments were also much more sophisticated than the elitist and reductionist views they are often accused of having, as, for example, John Durham Peters (2003) has argued in an insightful review of their culture industry essay. For example, few have noted the pronounced ambivalence of the very last sentence of the essay, in which the authors conclude that '[t]he triumph of advertising in the culture industry is that consumers feel compelled to buy and use its products even though they see through them' (Horkheimer and Adorno 1947/1994: 167). This is indeed a more complex view upon the effects of advertising than the simple hypodermic needle thesis this essay is often ascribed as having.

If this debate between cultural studies and political economy was at its height in the 1990s, the debate today has been reframed, not least due to the new media landscape we are facing. The buzzwords of the day are 'Web 2.0', 'creativity' and 'participation', with the discussion focussed on the increased opportunities on offer for media users to engage in productive aspects of media use. Whereas Web 1.0 brought with it an increased volume of texts to choose from, the basic structure was that of one-way communication. Web 2.0 opens new possibilities for dialogic communication, and for users to engage in social networking sites, wiki production, etc. In combination with smaller and more portable laptops, smartphones and tablet computers such as the iPad, coupled with increased wireless broadband access, this means that today many people – at least in the affluent West – can live their lives constantly online and on the move, making life effectively a 'media life' (Deuze 2009).

In a way, the Web 2.0 discussion is just a continuation of the active audience debate of earlier decades, for example the active audience in cultural studies, whereby a subdivision of the debate has concerned fan studies (for example, Lewis 1992, Hills 2002), and has been equipped with a partially new terminology, for instance 'participatory culture', a concept launched by Henry Jenkins (1992) in his highly influential work on the fans of *Star Trek*. Irrespective of the conceptual framework, however, the debate seems to rehash the question of whether audiences are active or passive, whether they are subjects or objects of the media and culture industry. 'The customer is not the king, as the culture industry would like to have us believe, not its subject but its object' would be Adorno's (1967/1975: 12) position in this debate, now as then, always emphasising the catastrophe rather than the utopia. The negative dialectics of Horkheimer and Adorno made them engage more vividly in the darker sides of modernity – although these negative phenomena were always the flip-side of the utopian possibilities. Adorno naturally did not live to see the advent of Web 2.0, or the digitalisation of culture. He would probably consider the consequences of digitisation his worst nightmare come true, or at least be engaged more enthusiastically in its description. But he would have also acknowledged the utopian possibilities inherent in the technological achievements.

However, there is another dimension to the argument on the relationship between the customer and the media and culture industries: If we take Adorno's quote seriously, we might say that it is not so much a question of ontology – whether we are the subject or the object of the media and culture industries. The ontological position will depend on which vantage point from which we are studying this relationship between media users and media industries. If we take a phenomenological user perspective, for example, it is perfectly legitimate to argue for agency on the part of the user. There is no doubt that he or she is active, creates meaning (and sometimes also textual expressions of a more sustainable kind), and is in this capacity a *produser*, in the words of Axel Bruns (for example, 2006, 2007); that is, a producing media user, one that is engaged in productive consumption, to use the concepts presented in Chapter 2. These phenomenological perspectives will naturally privilege concepts like 'produser', 'participation', 'user-generated content', 'creative industries', 'collective intelligence', 'crowdsourcing', 'distributed problem solving', etc. From a structural perspective, on the other hand, the very same activities stand out as restricted, circumscribed by constraints and limited choices, and instead of the concepts listed in the previous sentence we are presented with the phenomena in terms of 'exploitation', 'free labour', 'surveillance' and 'informational capitalism'. While neither of these perspectives is entirely wrong, neither of them alone does full justice to the entire process. In fact, few have discussed these phenomena as a 'both-and' issue, that is, as both an activity the user engages in, benefits from and values the use of and an activity that is then used by others for other ends and whereby other value forms are generated.

The polarisation between the activity emphasised by cultural studies on the one hand and the structural constraints on activity suggested by political economy on the other should, however, not be stressed too hard. As already mentioned in Chapter 2, an argument brought forth in the early political economy of television production was that audiences in commercial settings were indeed active, and that they were actually working in the service of networks while watching, contributing to the valorisation process of the capitalist media industry. This argument was originally put forth by Dallas Smythe (1977), and was further elaborated on by Sut Jhally and Bill Livant (1986). Already at that time, the view upon audiences as working for the networks was contested: As Eileen Meehan (1984) argued, audiences might not as much work for the industry as they are laboured upon as raw material in the production process (the real labour then being done by statisticians, producing audience ratings). This argument has lived on in contemporary debates in relation to television, for example by Mark Andrejevic, who has updated it 'for an era of new-media interactivity', in which media users 'self-disclose' details of their 'daily lives to increasingly pervasive and comprehensive forms of high-tech monitoring' (Andrejevic 2002: 231). This 'productive surveillance' feeds into the valorisation process, and is thereby to be regarded as labour for Andrejevic. His example in this early adoption and modification of the 'watching as working' discourse is TiVo, but in later works he has also extended the argument to techniques of location-based targeting and other database marketing technologies (Andrejevic 2007).

Following from this is that there are in fact two active audiences: one within the framework of political economy, and one within cultural studies. From the perspective of cultural studies, reception theory and media ethnography, it is argued that media users are undeniably productive, and that television viewing (and media engagement more generally) indeed has its outcomes. To the contrary of political economists such as Smythe and his followers, who consider the work of audiences within the framework of market economy, this type of production is of another kind, resulting in identities, taste cultures and social difference within the framework of social and cultural economies. The reasons for this insistence on the activity of the media user depart from a will to re-evaluate and reach beyond perceived elitist positions in which the activities of individual media users are depreciated. Following in the footsteps of the work of Janice Radway (1984/1987), Ien Ang (1982/1991) and other feminist reception researchers, as well as the micro-sociological work of Roger Silverstone (1994) and David Morley (1986), the interpretive work of viewers was taken seriously. Perhaps ironically, this research was modelled much on Stuart Hall's (1973) encoding-decoding model, which was indeed more than inspired by Marx's political economy and his production-consumption model in the discussion on method in the 1857 'Introduction' to *Grundrisse* (Marx 1939/1973: 81-111; see Hall 1974/2003). However, although its roots were in the politics of the economy, with the influences from Hall's encoding/decoding model it soon shifted focus to the politics of identity.

The Production of Social Difference

Within reception research and media ethnography, since the late 1970s and early 1980s it has been argued that media users are active, creative and far more critical than previously considered. The project of re-evaluation of the role of the media user is quite naturally sympathetic, and the political project to take 'ordinary' media users' thoughts, preferences and habits seriously is indeed of great importance. The task of this re-evaluation also follows quite naturally from the phenomenological perspectives media research imported from ethnomethodology, micro sociology, anthropology and ethnographic fieldwork. As such, ethnographic fieldwork aims at understanding one's informants' practices, or, to use the words of one of the pioneers of ethnographic media studies, James Lull: 'to allow the researcher to grasp as completely as possible with minimal disturbance the "native's perspective" on relevant communicative and sociocultural matters indigenous to him or her' (Lull 1980/1990: 31).

These phenomenological, ethnographic perspectives of understanding (*Verstehen*), often connected to cultural studies, were especially prominent within feminist and youth cultural research, and for good reason. One of the main motivations for research was to not see the female or youth media user as a problem to be solved due to their listening to daytime radio or watching television serials or horror films, but rather to take the 'native's perspective' in order to try to understand the meanings produced in reception, or better, in the encounter between an interpreting subject and media content. Through this production of meaning, social difference was also produced according to the various preferences, taste patterns and constructions of identities media users engaged in. In the next few paragraphs I will empirically relate to such a study, in order to show in detail some of the distinctive processes of media consumption.

The practice of watching horror and action films on video, mentioned in the previous paragraph, was actually the subject of my doctoral thesis (Bolin 1998). The thesis was based on fieldwork during the period of 1992 to 1996, during which I followed a small number of young male horror fans and their cultural consumption (watching huge amounts of slasher and stalker films on video) and production (fanzine writing and amateur film-making).[1] My interest focussed on the practices of the film swappers, as I came to call them on the grounds of their defining feature: swapping films on video with each other. This specific sort of cultural practice was born partly as a result of the introduction of a new media technology (video), and partly from the societal discussion of the films distributed (as 'video nasties'; cf. Barker 1984), also leading to a specific kind of legal discourse in the Swedish setting, that is, it became illegal to distribute some of the films that then circulated outside the official video rental market. The combination of these three features, I argue, can in fact help shed light on some of the processes we are witnessing today in the Web 2.0 digital era. Admittedly, the legal situation is specifically Swedish, but the new technology and the societal discourse on violent and culturally depreciated media content both have a wider international relevance. Although the film swappers' practices can be considered a quite specific pre-digital form of sharing media content, they nonetheless have relevance for our understanding of the consumption practices media users engage in today, in digital environments. The processes of producing difference, for example, are structurally similar at both points in time, as I will show, but there are also some notable new

---

1   The thesis itself is published in Swedish (Bolin 1998), but sections of it have been published in English in various fora. The most significant of these are Bolin (1994b, 1999, 2000).

features that have arrived with digitisation, which can improve our understanding of the changes digital technology has brought.

When it comes to media legislative frameworks, Sweden was the first country in the world to institutionalise national regulations for cinema in 1911, as a response to a fear that violent films could have a negative impact on the behaviour of youth, that is, that the young would become more violent (Skoglund 1971). Behind this concern were also arguments about foreign (that is, American) influences on Swedish culture. Thus, the National Swedish Board of Film Censors could be seen as having the dual purpose of keeping bad images, as well as bad cultural influences, out of the country. In the wake of a lengthy national debate on 'video nasties' in Sweden in the early 1980s, quite comparable with the British debate at around the same time, legislation prohibiting the dissemination of especially violent films on video was introduced. This meant that this specific repertoire of film subgenres within the framework of the broader action and horror categories disappeared from the shelves of video rental stores, and started to circulate among groups of predominantly young people, who for different reasons wanted to watch this media content. This phenomenon awoke my interest, for three reasons: firstly because these young men, the film swappers, made up a communicative structure formed around a common interest (to watch these films) that did not build on meeting each other face to face. In fact, of all my informants, who all had contact with each other through the swapping of films, no-one had met in person. Furthermore, they did not seem eager to do so either, as they were spread out across Sweden (although they used me as an informant regarding the other film swappers' activities). Secondly, I was interested in their practices of not only cultural consumption (watching huge amounts of films and swapping with each other) but also cultural production. All my informants were either producing fanzines or making amateur video films (naturally inspired by the genres they appreciated). This was in fact the basis for my choosing them as informants, and makes them naturally quite special. But as my interest was also in cultural production, and the specific ways consumption and production were related to one another, this was not a problem. My third interest in this phenomenon was their specific taste in films, their distinct reversal of all norms and criteria for aesthetic evaluation, and their insistence on the value of these subgenres' existence. Through this, they present a good example of the ways difference is produced in fields of consumption.

In fields of consumption, consumers consume objects and commodities that in the act of consumption produce difference. The way the consumer realises the sign value in the process of consumption produces a distinction from other consumers acting in the field. Distinction is thus produced socially, in relation to acts of consumption of specific objects and commodities invested with sign value, that is, the value that produces difference when realised in consumption. In the process of realisation, one and the same object can be consumed differently by different consumers. This also means that the act of consumption is an investment in the field that will supposedly lead to a prominent position within it, distinguished from other positions. As Bourdieu explains:

> [It is] the most risky but also the most profitable strategies of distinction, […] to constitute insignificant objects as works of art or, more subtly, to give aesthetic redefinition to objects as works of art, but in another mode, by other classes or class fractions (e.g. kitsch). In this case, it is the manner of consuming which creates the object of consumption, and a second-degree delight which transforms the 'vulgar' artefacts abandoned to common consumption […] into distinguished and distinctive works of culture. (Bourdieu 1979/1989: 282f)

These kinds of redefinitions of consumer products in consumption are common among fans of various kinds, the fan typically being a kind of consumer who invests heavily in consumption practices. The specific kinds of fans I studied – the film swappers – were, just like other fans, working very hard at their consumption, and they also undeniably directed their interest towards media content that others would consider 'insignificant' from an aesthetic point of view. This was naturally something the film swappers were quite aware of, and their film practices could be seen as a reversal of norms when it comes to the evaluation of films.

This reversal of aesthetic judgement naturally builds on the knowledge of legitimate taste and relates to a legitimate film culture and its cinematic canon. Although all the film swappers shared this reversed taste in relation to legitimate film culture, one could observe two basic ways of arguing cultural value – two distinct strategies, if you will. Firstly, there were those who clearly related to the legitimate cinematic canon, either by wanting to include the films they valued highly in an extension of the canon, or by wanting to replace the canon with their favourite films. The second strategy was a kind of rejection of canonisation as such, a refusal to make value judgements, and an apparent unpredictability of taste. This misrecognition of the field of aesthetic judgement, which is more in line with the strategy described by Bourdieu in the quote above, also led to those with this kind of taste being assigned the highest position within the field of the film swappers – indeed a very specific subfield, but nonetheless possible to analyse as a field of consumption.

A typical example of arguing cultural value from the first position is the following review from one of the fanzines:

> It's a weird piece, with the first full hour fully dedicated to hardcore sex only to turn into a splatter feast with various gore effects (mostly bad ones). The photography is clumsy, the story stinks like shit and the film has a really awful soundtrack by Nico Fidenco (remember that *Dr Butcher M.D*-theme?). But as with all films by Joe D'Amato it has a certain charm that's very hard to resist. It's ultra bad, but you'll love it anyway.[2]

---

2   Quote from the fanzine *Violent Vision*, no. 2 (1996): 36, English in original.

The author of this review discusses the film based on evaluative criteria from legitimate culture. He starts by placing the film within a genre system (hardcore sex and splatter films), then comments on formal features such as effects, photography, manuscript and sound (where he also gives intertextual references that establish a bond between reviewer and reader), and also points to the auteur status of the film's director, emphasising his own genre expertise by indicating his ability to judge this film in the light of the director's oeuvre. If one exchanged the specific genres and names and reversed the value judgements, this review could no doubt appear in the culture section of any daily newspaper. Although this reviewer and this faction of the film swappers have a deviant opinion on what is to be considered good taste, the forms for evaluating cultural objects within legitimate culture are generally accepted: the focus on formal features, production values, and so on.

The more distinctive way of consuming, and letting others know of one's way of consuming, can be represented by the following quote, from the fanzine *Black*:

> I'm not really sure what I see in blaxploitation films that I like so damn much. I'm white, I don't listen to soul of any kind and I'm not American. Some of the films have a very high turkey value and I have always enjoyed a good turkey, the jive is also a very important ingredient, it took some time to appreciate it, but now I love it, it's great. The action is many times more violent than in standard action films and since I'm a sucker for cheap gore, violence, nudity I get all this in these films (not all, but many). the flashy 70's clothing these studs often use is also incredibly groovy, big collars to shocking flares and on top of that a dangerous hat in the latest pimp fashion!
>
> As you understand I can never see the films in the same perspective as the blacks must do, they live in the ghetto and they are the ones pushed around by "The man", they probably have more respect to these films. In spite of all, I'm just a confused white sleazy guy enjoying this for the fun of it.[3]

Although revealing a highly reflexive stance, this fanzine editor (who signs his articles 'Dr. Black' and is the driving force behind the production of the fanzine) does not try to discuss formal features, although the opportunity lies close at hand when he mentions the 'turkey' value of blaxploitation films. He rather dwells on the expressive (and excessive) aesthetics (although he does not discuss these from a formal perspective either), whereby the key expressions 'groovy' and 'fun' can be related to emotional rather than intellectual experiences. It is the subjective impact of the film that is emphasised, but a subjective impact that cannot be explained sociologically in terms of ethnic, class or national identification. The points of identification that are emphasised are all aesthetic – the jive, the stylish clothing, the violence and nudity portrayed, etc. This strategy does not aim at changing any

---

3   Quote from the fanzine *Black* no. 12 (1992), 22. English in original.

cinematic canon. The author does not make an argument for why this genre should be considered legitimate, and the text ends in an unresolved contention that he cannot answer the question posed at the beginning. It lies unresolved as a mystery, freed from any social or moral concern. The value of the film is not grounded in the social, the educational, the political, but rather in the disinterested aesthetical impression the film gives him.

Another highly distinctive move Dr. Black and the co-writers of his fanzines made, and the one that is really modelled after Bourdieu's quote above, was to suddenly reveal a taste for mainstream media content. In a field of consumption where everyone tries to display their knowledge about the most hard-to-find copies of legendary slasher films (and we must remember that this was before the digital expansion in which everything is just a mouse-click away), the 'most risky but also the most profitable' strategy is to embrace mainstream culture, as indicated by his 'confession':

> Hi, thought I'd write a review for this film. Well, it didn't turn out that way. The fact is that I happened to overwrite it with a documentary about Siamese twins on TV4. Sitting here now listening to Springsteen feeling kind of silly. Wonder what I'll tell the guy I borrowed the tape from …[4]

In this specific field of consumption centred on the preference for extremely violent action and horror films in which legitimate and mainstream taste is reversed, the most powerful act of consumption is to display this obviously mainstream taste in music (Bruce Springsteen), and in the most mainstream of all media technologies: television (a documentary on the most mainstream commercial broadcasting channel in Sweden, TV4). Although the author is careful in displaying his careless attitude in relation to his overwriting the film he was supposed to review, the very fact that this statement is published in a fanzine with a circulation among hardcore fans of the most violent and gory films reveals that this is actually a stake in the social game of producing difference by consuming sign value. Through the refusal to conform to the common taste within the field, seemingly standing above or beyond such 'conformism of anti-conformism' (Bourdieu and Passeron 1964/1979: 46), one also secures an autonomous position as free from all constraints when it comes to value judgements, in fact displaying the ability to adopt a pure aesthetic gaze on the seemingly most non-significant objects of consumption. Indeed, this is how 'the manner of consuming', as Bourdieu puts it, 'creates the object of consumption'. This is the interplay between the individual in a consumption structure (field), whereby the meeting between the individual and the field produces both the individual's position in the field as well as the value, the very quality that comes to be struggled over.

---

4 Quote from the fanzine *Salong Finess* no. 2 (1996): 5, my translation from the Swedish. *Salong Finess* was the fanzine he started after *Black*, when blaxploitation films gained popularity.

This position can only be acquired by constructing a belief among the other agents within the field that one does not care whether the objects one prefers or values are valued positively by others. This denial of the existence of the game can also be considered an attempt at evading or *escaping* the field, which in fact puts the attempting escapee in a more elevated position *within* the field, since all opinions and evaluations, including the refusal to evaluate, are evaluated by others in the end. And the most distinguished positions are acquired by those who can make the other agents in the field believe they need not evaluate, that they do not care about evaluation, that is, that they have acquired total autonomy and are unrestricted in their choices.

An argument against such an interpretation might be that this subfield of consumption is so specific that it has no relevance for the evaluation of the principles of value judgement within more legitimate areas. However, one should acknowledge that all fields have been embryonic at one point in time, even that of literature in France in the late 19th century, one of the main examples used by Bourdieu (1992/1996). A striking parallel to the example of the most distinctive film swappers formed around the fanzine *Black*, which I have accounted for above, can be found in the subtle analysis by Staffan Ericson (2004) of the strategies employed by August Strindberg in his strive towards an autonomous status within the literary field, first in France (Paris), which means the very same field Bourdieu analyses, and then in Sweden (Stockholm) shortly after the turn of the last century. After having outraged, disappointed and/or made enemies of all his former colleagues, competitors and friends through the publication in 1907 of *Svarta fanor* (published in English as *Black Banners*, Strindberg 1907/2010), a key novel in which he 'settles accounts' with key figures in the literary field of Stockholm and accordingly provokes scandal, he writes about the effects of the publication: 'That my repeated confessions were not taken seriously is not my fault. […] Then I was forced to gradually speak more clearly until I explained myself in Black Banners with no possibility of misunderstanding. Then I was understood, and thus I was free!' (quoted in Ericson 2004: 118, my translation). In his analysis of Strindberg's strivings to gain recognition, Ericson accounts for how Strindberg with this move acquires his distinct autonomous position by 'applying for resignation from the field' (Ericson 2004: 122). The most effective way to play the game, accordingly, is to convincingly claim that one does not wish to play it.

In order to have a strong effect in the field, a strong distinctive power, the symbolic value of the commodities struggled over must be distinct, and worth the while and engagement to argue over. This means that the more controversial this value is, the harsher the discussion and arguments will be over its worth (or worthlessness), and the higher the stakes for arguing this value. This is why highly controversial media content has a higher significance in such discussions than mainstream content. It is naturally possible for consumers to argue over preferences for this or that reality show, say *Strictly Come Dancing*, *Survivor*, *Paradise Hotel*, or an entertainment lottery game show such as Swedish format *Bingolotto*, but these are far from as controversial as extremely violent and gory horror films with bad production value (that is, 'bad' according to legitimate evaluative standards). To be able to transform lowly esteemed objects, to 'constitute insignificant objects as works of art' as Bourdieu puts it, is a more profitable strategy, and one that has been successfully adopted by current renowned film-maker Quentin Tarantino, incidentally sharing my informant's taste for blaxploitation films. When Tarantino's popularity increased and he openly paid homage to the blaxploitation genre with *Jackie Brown* (1997), my informant Dr. Black had already several years previously abandoned this taste for 1970s action films with black actors, and was currently instead engaged in a more controversial but also more distinctive media content: Swedish amateur pornography, especially films lacking the functional dimension of most regular pornographic films of stimulating sexual arousal. When he did so, no other film swapper followed, although they all declared their admiration for this obviously crazy preference in films. Again, one can see parallels with Strindberg's attempts at being successful in the literary field of France in the late 19th century, publishing essays and plays that would have his readers discussing his possible growing insanity, an apprehension that Strindberg also eagerly (but secretly) fuelled. 'This is just crazy enough to be considered modern', he reflected in a letter to a friend back in Sweden on one of his essays, published in *Le Figaro* in 1894 as an attempt at entering the French (Parisian) literary field (Ericson 2004: 68; my translation).

Admittedly, the examples of Strindberg and Tarantino do not relate to fields of cultural consumption but rather to fields of production. However, as I have already emphasised, the fields of consumption and production have a structural similarity, which can be explained by their being dialectical pieces of the same production-consumption process. Furthermore, writers like Strindberg and film and television directors like Tarantino are naturally themselves consumers of cultural artefacts. In fact, it would be very difficult to act in a field of cultural production if you did not consume and engage in the cultural production of your competitors. The ability to navigate, the very capacity to master the game of the field, builds on the minute knowledge about the other agents (the competitors), the important institutions, and the cultural genres that circulate, and of course the displayed sensibility in relation to the value at stake. To Bourdieu, being a sociologist, this is not an ability one is born with. As pointed out in Chapter 2, Bourdieu holds the view that capital 'is accumulated labor (in its materialised form or its "incorporated" form)' (Bourdieu 1983/1986: 241). Positions acquired within a field do not come to you by chance; They are the result of hard work and training, until the ability to orient within the field is 'incorporated' into a person's *habitus* – the acquired disposition to act in the field. This goes for the field of consumption as well as that of production. In fact, the field model and its insistence on the active production of belief presuppose that one works to uphold this belief that the field is centred on. The work of production is then structurally similar to that of consumption.

In the pre-digital era of fanzine writing and amateur video-making, the work of consumption was mostly carried out on objects that were tangible (but were the bearers of substantial sign value), that is, printed fanzines and copied videocassettes.

These were circulated in informal networks of distribution, and under conditions that the consumers/producers – especially in the case of the film swappers – themselves controlled. In the age of digital reproduction and distribution, the work of consumption involves non-tangible objects and commodities. Contemporary fans would not produce printed fanzines, or distribute their amateur films on videocassettes. They would simply use the Internet as the platform of distribution, and the computer as the means of consumption. And adding to this, they would produce discussion threads and post their fan fiction on fan websites, or share links to other sites of possible interest to other media users. The significance of this shift will be revisited in the last section of this chapter, but first let us turn for a moment to a more elaborate discussion on the kinds of work that are involved in consumption and media use.

The Work of Media Use and Consumption

In the interview material I have on the film swappers, there is an account of a situation in which my informant Dr. Black was asked what he worked with. His reply was '*Black* – that is my work. Then I spend eight hours each day doing some other crap. But that's just to be able to afford to do my work' (Bolin 1998: 178). This statement indicates that the concept of work is also a stake in the game of producing difference. Referring to an activity as work thus means conferring value on that activity, to signify importance. What Dr. Black is telling the interviewer is that the thing he spends eight hours a day with is insignificant, unimportant, and an effort he puts up with in order to engage in the activity he values more highly: watching and reviewing films on video and putting his fanzine together. It is not a hobby, not an enthusiasm, but work.

Work as an activity, however, can obviously mean several things, although at its foundation it always presupposes that it is productive, it results in something. The character of this 'something' can vary substantially, however, and one way to characterise it could be in terms of subjective, social and textual work. Obviously all media users are involved in *subjective work*, that is, the construction of thoughts, ideas, emotions, and reflections that result from media use. This is the subjective production of meaning for the individual media user. When these thoughts, ideas, emotions, etc., are communicated to others, the work of constructing meaning becomes *social*, that is, it becomes a shared production of meaning. Thirdly, it can take manifest form in an individually or collectively produced text. This is the production of meaning through *textual work*, for example in the form of amateur videos, narratives, songs, paintings or fanzines. The result of this third kind of work is more manifest and less transient.

At least, this was the case before the age of digital production and reproduction. Before digitisation the possibilities to produce one's own media content were indeed more restricted, and more comparable with the production of tangible commodities. The industrial production of culture did not, at least in some respects, differ much from the industrial production of material/tangible objects and commodities. You could simply not start producing cars, vacuum cleaners or refrigerators on a mass scale without strong financial back-up. Cultural production also required high levels of initial investment, and access to means of production that were usually far too expensive for the ordinary media user to acquire if he or she wanted to turn to production. This was especially so with professional cultural production, but amateur production could also involve high initial economic thresholds. Aspiring musicians, say a couple of friends who wanted to make a recording of good quality, had to hire time in a recording studio to make a demo tape, which they would later present to record companies in the hope that they would find it interesting enough to put up the money for studio time for the recording of a full-length album. The same goes for film production, which quite quickly developed into an industry with high initial costs and great uncertainties when it comes to return on investment. Already from the start there was a division between professional and amateur formats, with 35 or 70mm becoming the professional standard and 8mm the amateur standard (with 16mm somewhere in between) (Zimmermann 1995: 21ff). The examples could also be extended to other areas: television, publishing, journalism. In most of these areas there has existed a distinction between professional and amateur formats.

Today, however, the aspiring musician has the technological means to produce high quality recordings in the home. Since the introduction of the relatively inexpensive portastudio in the late 1970s, and the introduction of editing software for personal computers in the early 1990s (Thebérge 1997: 220ff), costs for music production with good technical quality have shrunk dramatically. For the young pop star *in spe* it is no longer an insurmountable economic risk to start producing his or her own music and then distribute it on MySpace or other similar sites. The costs of production are low, and the costs of distribution even less. The technology, quite naturally, cannot compensate for lack of talent, but undeniably makes it easier for musicians to record and edit their own music. The young journalist can start his or her own blog, and indeed quite a few do; The technological equipment for producing your own short film is within the economic reach of most enthusiasts, as are editing programmes for computers – you can post your novel or display your photo art on the Internet, etc. Again, technology does not compensate for talent, but the technological means of production and dissemination are there to be taken advantage of.

Through digitisation, then, the means for engaging in social and textual work have increased tremendously. The difference is not only quantitative, in that we have more platforms to communicate with each other on. In addition to face-to-face communication and the landline telephone, we have a range of other technologies at our disposal in the form of the personal and pervasive media we carry with us all the time (mobile phones, laptops, etc.). However, the difference is also qualitative. The social work of consumption that today takes advantage of the communicative possibilities of social networking sites and web fora also instantly becomes textual work through these digital technologies. And this work leaves material remains in the digital environment. These remains might not last forever, but they will certainly exist longer than the mere enunciation of a value judgement. When we orally discuss the qualities of a television drama, the experience of playing a computer game, or the new release by Lady Gaga, these are value judgements that are transient, living on only as memories among the co-present discussants. But when we engage in the same evaluations on Facebook or any other social networking site, this conversation has the possibility to reach far more partakers, and for a longer period of time. This is indeed one of the major shifts digitisation brings; the gradual expansion of value judgements one can join in, criticise or just observe. In a very material way, then, the means of consumption, the technologies by which we consume images and sound, also instantly provide us with the means of production of social evaluation and judgement (and the production of difference). In a way, then, social work and textual work merge, as social work is also conflated with the textual work of uploading pictures on social networking sites, sending files to friends and family, relaying viral marketing messages in the form of amusing video clips, etc.

Work, as it was conceptualised within cultural studies, reception theory and media ethnography, was never related to the valorisation process. It was rather used metaphorically, for example in combination with activities such as interpretation, as in 'interpretive work', or related to processes of identity formation, as in 'identity work'.

Identity work was a common concept especially in youth cultural research, where it was adopted from the German social psychologist and leading inspiration for Nordic youth culture research, Thomas Ziehe (1982/1986: 25f). Ziehe's point was to emphasise the struggle young people had to go through in late modern society, where identities were not inherited from generation to generation like it (supposedly) was in earlier days. In late modern society, argues Ziehe, young people are more free to choose among a variety of different identity positions to the contrary of their parents, who were more restrained in their choices. However, this is not only freedom of choice. Since identities are not inherited to the extent they were before, the young person is not only free to choose – he or she also *has to* choose. The dialectical opposite of the freedom to choose one's future identity position was also the enforced pressure on the young person to actively reflect on and choose from the seemingly endless choices at hand, many of which were provided by the media. Identity does not arrive automatically and inherently. The individual has to be active in the construction of his or her identity, to work at it. To Ziehe, identity work is thus an individual category, tied to the subject in a socialisation process that is increasingly open to the individual.

From a more constructivist sociological point of view, identity work was used in a British context by Stanley Cohen and Laurie Taylor (1976/1992), as a way to capture the everyday effort involved in shaping one's identity. The specific case Cohen and Taylor discuss is the identity work of long-term prisoners. These are 'people who by their behaviour set themselves apart from others – declared themselves to be different' (p. x). The interesting thing about the identity work of long-term prisoners, argue Cohen and Taylor, is that 'the symbolic resources for differentiation were scarce' (p. 41). Whereas the young people Ziehe describes struggle with their identities by adopting specific styles from the endless catalogue provided by the mass media, these are not tools available to prisoners, and accordingly prisoners have to work on their differentiation in more subtle ways. The common denominator between the identity work of the two groups that Cohen and Taylor and Ziehe describes is the struggle for difference, by analogy the same work that is carried out in less spectacular situations among everyday consumers, consuming commodities loaded with sign value.

From a similar constructivist position, Paul Willis (1990: 9ff) used the concepts of 'symbolic work' and 'symbolic creativity' to describe youth cultural practices, a kind of work he sees as an inherently 'necessary' part of 'everyday human activity'. The basic elements or resources of such symbolic work are, among other things, language ('the primary instrument by which we communicate'), the active body (the 'site of somatic knowledge'), drama ('dancing, singing, joke-making, story-telling in dynamic settings and in performance'), and, lastly, 'symbolic creativity', a category that seemingly encompasses the three others in combination (Willis 1990: 11). It is through this creativity that individual identities are produced and reproduced.

In sum, all these aspects of media use are undeniably to be justified as work. This work, as I have argued, can be subjective, social or textual. However, with digitisation the status of social work changes in relation to the media and culture industries. If social work in the pre-digital era was more like subjective work, with the advent of digitisation it has become more like textual work, and in this capacity it has become possible for the industries to appropriate it. In the next section we shall see the consequences of this on the productive consumption of digital media use.

The Productive Consumption of the Digital Media User

A consequence of the focus on the active, interpreting subject in reception theory and media ethnography was the very conceptualisation of the activity of media users in terms of symbolic work, identity work and interpretive work, but also in textual work and fan production, a discussion that has lived on in discourses on audience creativity and convergence culture. Historically, this re-evaluation of the media user can be seen as a reaction to the view on audiences as passive masses at the prey of ideological messages. This re-evaluation can be paralleled to the re-evaluation of domestic, female household work. The late 1970s and early 1980s saw growing feminist criticism of the neglect and depreciation of female domestic work. As Nancy Folbre (1982) argues, the blind spot in Marxian labour theory of value was that the wage worker needed to consume the labour power of others in order to reproduce his (as it was most often the case in Marx's days that the worker was male) own labour power, and that unpaid, unrecognised labour was never accounted for in the valorisation process within the framework of capitalist production. The fact that domestic labour is unrecognised in Marxian theory masks processes of exploitation within the home, argues Folbre, as only the labour that relates directly to the accumulation of capital is seen as exploitation (not the reproduction of the breadwinner's labour power to which the female household worker contributes) (cf. Streeter 1996: 291ff). This shift in focus indeed has its consequences, in that an area of our lifeworlds that was previously considered outside the market economy has been drawn into it. In this respect, domestic work also becomes commodified and subsumed by the logics of the market. In the same way as industrial labour is made up of the working power of the (male) factory worker, domestic labour becomes a commodity.

When Jhally and Livant argue that television viewers are actually working for the networks while watching, this is seemingly a similar move that attempts to incorporate the leisure time of media users into the production-consumption circuit, thus extending the area that is subsumed by capitalist production. Through this, an attempt is made to bestow the watching of television with value by insisting that it actually contributes to the valorisation process, whereby it is to be considered 'the peculiar commodity', labour (Marx 1867/1976: 274).

One of the basic problems with the 'watching as working' perspective of Smythe, Jhally and Livant and others was, as argued in previous chapters, that they confused audience statistics with the actual labour of media users. Audiences do not work; It is rather the statisticians and market executives who do. It is these people who decide on the formal procedures, the techniques and methodologies by which the audience statistics are tooled into a commodity. In fact, this model for analysing audience work does not work (sic) for television broadcasting, as the statistical aggregate cannot be linked back to social users. It might be argued that the only viewers who work are those on the Nielsen ratings panel, as their individual uses of television actually have an impact on the commodity produced: the aggregated audience statistics. But even this individual viewing would not be worth anything to networks if this consumption were not managed and tooled into the audience commodity by statisticians.

Audiences also do not produce meaning, identities or cultural tastes (at best, these are constructed as preferences and/or lifestyle patterns in audience segmentation analysis). However, media users do. And in the pre-digital era, these identities belonged to the media users themselves and could not be appropriated and drawn into the production process by the media and culture industries. They could not circulate in a field of cultural production – only in the field of cultural consumption, producing difference. However, with digitisation they can. The above-described act of social work and communication on social networking sites does indeed contribute to the media user's identity and the meaning produced in consumption though value judgements that previously in the pre-digital era was the media user's own, but that in the digital economy becomes appropriated as 'free labour' (Terranova 2000) by the media and culture industries. This labour is not only 'free', as in not paid for by the industries, but is also freely submitted by media users in the digital economy – media users experiencing 'niche envy' (Turow 2006), consumers who 'feel compelled to buy and use [the media industries'] products even though they see through them' (Horkheimer and Adorno 1947/1994: 167).

Smythe, Jhally, Livant and Meehan developed their arguments in a pre-digital media world, just as early active audience theory was developed in cultural studies. The analogy of media use as labour only fits that world insofar as it refers to fields of cultural consumption, where consumers labour on the consumption of commodities, and through this realise sign value (and in so doing, produce difference). This produced difference realised in the consumption of sign value was very hard for the media and culture industries to take advantage of. It resided in the consumer as an asset, in the same way as labour power resides in the worker as 'capacity for labour' (Marx 1867/1976: 270), a capacity that can be set in motion and sold as a commodity. The meanings and identities produced in consumption were, however, very hard to convert into this capacity in a way that would make them desired by the media and culture industries.

With digitisation, all this changes. The traffic commodity, as described in Chapter 3, undisputedly has its base in the activities of real social users, who, as Andrejevic (2002) holds, 'work at being watched', and makes it possible for the media industries to tailor advertising messages that fit their specific behaviour. In this sense the analogy of working at being watched proposed by Andrejevic is much more fitting than the 'watching as working' hypothesis.

This specific kind of labour has at times been labelled 'immaterial labour' by autonomist Marxists scholars (Dyer-Witheford 1999, Lazzarato 1996, Virno 1996). This is the labour 'that produces an immaterial product, such as ideas, images, forms of communication, affects, or social relationships' (Hardt 2005: 176). The concept is misleading, as it is not labour but rather the result of labour that is immaterial (and as I argued previously, intangible is a better concept than immaterial in relation to the media). The activity of working is just as material irrespective of the outcome of the labour process. Constructing media texts out of the combination of signs, that is, engaging in signifying practices in the labour of signification, does not differ from physical work. The labourer sells his labour capacity irrespective of whether that capacity builds on physical strength or intellectual capabilities.

***

In a way the two active audiences, as they were theorised in the pre-digital world of media production and consumption, were acting in two specific fields of production and consumption. The active audience of cultural studies, reception theory and media ethnography acted in a field of consumption together with and in relation to other consumers, producing difference, distinction, identity and culture – things that were difficult to mediate into fields of cultural production, where the active agents were professional media and culture producers (television stations, publishers, computer game producers, music promoters, curators, etc.). Although the work in fields of consumption is not only 'symbolic' in terms of subjective or social work but at times also materialises in textual works (fanzines, amateur film-making, etc.), even these tangible outcomes of consumption-production practices were hard for the industries to take advantage of. And although some fanzine authors were able to develop skills that were convertible into labour capacity within the field of production, this indicates more that the fields of consumption were training grounds, self-directed educational fora where one could develop skills to be used elsewhere.

With digitisation, the relationship between fields of production and fields of consumption changes, as digitisation makes some of these processes accessible in fields of production. Firstly, in digital environments the media user acts in the field of consumption, producing difference as well as aesthetic and social value through subjective and, most importantly, social labour. The activity that produces difference, aesthetic and social value is then appropriated by the media and culture industries as labour in order to produce exchange value. Secondly, the textual work of active audiences and fans that results in user-generated content (to use the Web 2.0 discourse) is also appropriated by the industry. Hence, as Peter Jakobsson and Fredrik Stiernstedt (2010) have shown, this produces the ambivalent attitude on the part of the industry, which on on the one hand deplores the difficulties involved in protecting one's own commodities (media content in the form of music, films, computer games) and on the other hand denies the rights of the 'user-generators' who actually fill Facebook, MySpace and other networking sites with content the return on *their* investment: the wages for their labour.

Yochai Benkler's (2006) massively influential book *The Wealth of Networks* departs from the observation that the production of information, knowledge and culture has long been marked by 'non-market' motivations, in contrast to the production of other industrially produced commodities such as cars. In addition to this observation, Benkler argues that a 'structural change' has occurred, whereby this kind of production is of greater importance today. Furthermore, he also observes a tendency towards an increase in 'large-scale cooperative efforts' in the production of information and culture (Benkler 2006: 4f). However, although he is right in his observation that there have indeed been some profound changes in cultural production over the past decades, his insistence on the 'cooperative efforts' also misrecognises the fact that we are dealing with two kinds of production practices, with two different outcomes: the production of difference on the one hand and the production of capital on the other.

Providing an analytical research account is a constructivist practice: As a researcher, you also produce the producing cultures that are the result of ethnographic accounts. Whether the cultures that are the focus of study are described as being engaged in production (rather than consumption), 'cooperative' or, indeed, passive masses is the result of choices made by the researcher in his or her analytical work. In the above I have proposed a different model for understanding the changed character of the production-consumption circuits, and in the next chapter I will focus more specifically on the sign commodity that circulates in these fields of consumption and production.

Chapter 5
New Textual Expressions and Patterns of Narration

The previous two chapters have each focussed on some of the consequences of the twin processes of digitisation and marketisation. Chapter 3 discussed the rise of new as well as not so new business models that have been launched in the wake of digitisation, and the consequences for the generation of value that these models bring with them. An organisational feature in this process is that media companies have become tightly diversified in large-scale media houses, or have engaged in tie-ins that are supposedly mutually beneficial to all parties involved, for example business models that build on co-operations between ISPs, search engine optimisers and advertisers. Besides these two corporate strategies one could add another strategy, connected to the marketisation process: the television format business, in which media content production is diversified to meet the challenges of the international distribution of content. Many of the most successful television formats that are distributed internationally have been in reality genres, building on viewer engagement and participation (through voting, for example), thus drawing media consumers into the production process.

Chapter 4 presented a discussion of some of the changed roles of producers and consumers in the valorisation process that appear in the fields of media and cultural production and consumption. A technological feature of these processes of change is that the means of consumption also have become the means of production, making it possible for media users to take part in the production of media content in new ways. In the above-mentioned format business, we can see one form of such contributions to the production of content as part of the changing role of media users.

These changed roles, and the changes in the media and culture industries in general, have in certain respects affected media content. In the wake of these changes we can see new possibilities for narrative constructions and genre development due to the ability to combine stories across technological platforms, such as television, the web and mobile phones. Such new textual expressions and patterns of narration will be the focus of this chapter, where firstly the phenomenon of the television format as a part of institutional and market convergence will be discussed. As many television formats include the active use of web and mobile phone services, the second part of the chapter will be devoted to a discussion of the new textual features connected to such multiplatform media production.

Rationalising International Media Content: The Television Format

As argued above, digitisation has made the distribution of media content easier, not only when it comes to geographical spread across nations but also across technological platforms. Geographical dissemination is hardly a new feature, and in small countries where the domestic market is insufficient for commercial production, one has had to rely either on state subsidies, as has long been the case with the Swedish film industry, or on cross-national co-productions. In the Nordic setting, it is thus common to co-produce feature films with the help of the fellow Nordic film and television companies, and we have also seen Nordic co-production of television series involving actors and directors, for example the police series *Örnen* (The Eagle, 2004-2006), a co-production involving the Swedish, Danish, Norwegian, Icelandic and German public service broadcasters.

Such rationalisation of film production is not new, but it poses a language problem for national audiences. In the early 1930s, following the increased costs of film production after the introduction of sound, and with the knowledge that audiences prefer domestic films in their own national languages, Paramount initiated 'multi-language' film production in Paris. The idea was to make several national adaptations of the same manuscript, using the same stage, props and equipment, but to have teams of national directors and actors executing the film, thus using the same formula for different national markets. Hence, teams of Swedish directors, actors and actresses travelled to Paris to shoot films, which were then premiered at the Swedish theatres. Already the first year of production (1930) saw the production of 150 films in 14 different language versions, according to Swedish film historian Per Olov Qvist (1994: 42). The production was industrialised, and logistically entailed that the film teams travelled from Sweden to Paris, shot the film in one or two days, and then returned to Sweden. Each scene in the film was filmed in national variants, which meant that there could be several film production units present at one time. Qvist quotes Swedish actress Inga Tidblad, who in an interview vividly retells the procedure when shooting a scene with the co-presence of a German and French production team:

> In order to save film, all three Fannies [the character Fanny] were lined up in the harbour where they were supposed to run out on the pier and shout 'Marius'. There we were, all three of us, in exactly the same aprons and the same fishmonger hats. We could barely keep from laughing when it was commanded 'Camera! Action!'. First off was the German Fanny shouting 'Mariuss!', and then the French one with her 'Mari-uss', and then the Swedish one – well, that was me. (*Svensk Filmografi* 1973: 103, my translation)

The reception among film critics in Sweden was not overwhelmingly positive, although some of the films were successful with audiences. Most of them, however, were economic failures and did not meet with approval among audiences (Qvist 1994: 45). Ginette Vincendeau (1988) has argued that the main reason for the failure was that the manuscripts, with their Hollywood origin, were too far removed from the generic traditions within the various European national contexts. Thus, language alone was not enough. One should have tried to adapt the different versions more to the different regional traditions of film-making to have had a chance for success.

Arguably, the global media market was not ripe for multi-language productions like those initiated by Paramount. However, since the late 1990s we have seen the rise of a similar model of production: the television format. As the example of multi-language films shows, this kind of rationalisation of production leads to changes in the textual features – in this case Swedish films (as well as French, German and British ones, etc.). And not all of these changes meet with the approval of the viewers. The format has been launched as a solution to this problem.

The concept of format is used in a variety of ways in different contexts, not least in relation to different media technologies. On the one hand, then, the uses of the concept shift according to which medium is discussed, and on the other, between different users in relation to the same medium. The concept is possible to break down into at least four main dimensions, which will be discussed in this section:

- as a technical form (technical format)
- as a programme form (programme format)
- as a logic for organising schedules and audience flows (channel format)
- as a commodity (commodity format)

Firstly, the concept of format is historically a technical term, connected to the technology of printing. Within this context it used to refer to the size of the pages of a book, based on the 'manner in which a sheet of paper is or is not folded to end up as the "leaves" of a book' (that is, the book's pages) or 'the size of the original sheet itself' (Genette 1987/1997: 17). A more recent counterpart can be found within film production, where it defines a range of different celluloid formats of production, storage and projection. In the early film industry one distinguished between 8, 16 and 35 mm film, and with the arrival of video, formats such as Betavideo, Digibeta, Video-8, VHS and DVD have developed. Over the 20th century, music was distributed on EP, LP, Compact Cassettes (CC), CDs, and recently also in non-tangible, digital MP3 formats that can be stored on several tangible carriers (cf. Wikström 2006: 165ff). When it comes to the press we can find the concept of format connected to the different sizes of newspapers: broadsheet, Berliner or tabloid, etc., formats. To the contrary of the case of film, whereby a certain format indicated amateurism or professionalism (cf. Zimmermann 1995: 21ff), one does not speak of amateur formats within the press (if, perhaps, not A4 format as a fanzine format). When it comes to computers we also have formats (for example, we format discs, CDs, DVDs), and with our Word or Powerpoint programs we format templates, etc. When it comes to formats as technical terms, it is quite obvious that these are connected to the specificities of each individual media technology, although we can see that some media are technologically converging, such as film and music, which can both be laid down on video tapes and DVDs. We therefore cannot automatically apply a format discussion within one medium to another. However, in this context in which we focus on television as a medium, we can disregard press, film, video and computer formats. And if it is indeed possible to talk of various formats when it comes to the size of the television screen, or to HDTV, these are hardly the most important or interesting features concerning our understanding of television as a medium.

Secondly, and more crucial to the discussion on format in the broadcast media, format can be used to describe *programme forms*, as a conceptual tool for the production of different types of television (and radio) programmes. Adopted in this way one can see the concept of format as close to the genre concept, perhaps as a subcategory of it. The concept of genre seems to also sometimes be used as equivalent to format. Genres can be seen as a kind of formula (Cawelti 1976), or a code (Berger 1992), that organises apprehensions and practices surrounding the production, distribution and consumption of texts. Genres are both descriptive of and prescriptive for how a certain text is given meaning in the circuit of production and consumption. Genres, however, also develop and change over time within the context of an institutional and social practice – they are historically situated negotiations between the producers and users of media texts (cf. Neale 1980, 1990). These generic conventions seem to shift more in television compared to those in literature and cinema, perhaps also in music, although musical genres are also in constant flux. In relation to the concept of format one could, for example, hold that the genre 'talk show' encompasses several formats such as current affairs, infotainment, etc. They all have certain characteristics in common (a programme host, a studio, conversations, etc.), but they also differ to a certain extent in how they are structured and represented: The range of topics is varied, the hosts act differently, infotainment programmes often have artists in the studio and a studio audience, etc.

Thirdly, one can talk about *channel format*. This is especially so for radio, which has developed to indicate a channel profile distinguishable from other radio channels or stations with which one competes for listeners to sell to advertisers or their agents (Berland 1990). This usually involves the systematic use of specific music (sub)genres, a specific audience address, jingles and other markers which are supposed to give the channel a specific channel identity, supposedly marking it off from the surrounding competitive environment. Sometimes this struggle by commercial broadcasters for distinction from other channels produces unintended effects. An audible trend in Sweden has been that the commercial radio stations have worked hard to profile themselves against the public service stations (of which there are five, plus a range of digital channels), which paradoxically has led to the fact that the most easily distinguishable channels *are* the public service ones, since they individually have their specific content (P1 = talk radio; P2 = classical music; P3 = youth radio that typically avoids playing the rotated music that defines the playlists of all commercial channels; P4 = regional broadcasts;

and finally P5 = local radio, mainly in the larger cities). As the commercial radio channels in Sweden and the Nordic countries (and partly also those in the Baltic countries) are owned by the same companies, it is also easy to identify their Nordic (Baltic) counterparts within each channel format. For example, the commercial radio channel Rix FM has its counterpart in Estonia, Latvia and Lithuania in the channel Star FM, and all are run by the Swedish-based media conglomerate Modern Times Group (MTG) (Stiernstedt 2008). Not only is their rotated music the same (AC, or Adult Contemporary), they have identical jingles, disc jockeys who address the same imaginary 'P1' listener (the listener who has Rix FM/Star FM as her favourite radio station, and not to be confused with the public service radio channel P1) – a 33-year-old woman with two children living a married life in the suburbs, working in an office, playing sports twice a week, shopping at large supermarkets and driving a five-year-old leased car – and even identical graphical profiles on their web pages, with similar logotypes, etc. (Forsman and Stiernstedt 2006).

The medium of television has not developed as refined format forms in this respect, perhaps because television has a larger repertoire of symbolic cues, and can combine both sound and image. In this respect television can rely on the channel marker in the top left or right corner of the television screen, which automatically signals to the viewer what channel he/she is watching, and which leaves greater freedom for varying the audience address within the scope of every individual channel. MTV, CNN, Discovery Nature/History, etc., and other concept channels can, however, be said to be format channels in the same way as format radio channels are. But other television channels also use modes of address, graphics and other markers to aid in the profiling of the channel. On the basis of a conceptual core, these and other components are developed and redesigned in a continuous strive to reach the target audience and to predict and plan its viewing patterns. Format logic is, then, intimately connected to scheduling (Ytreberg 2001). A programme or channel format is never written in stone, however, but instead changes over time. This is the case partly because 'novelty' in itself is an attractive value for every channel (new features, new set designs or graphics, new guests, etc.), and it can partly be ascribed to the fact that extra-textual premises can change between seasons, for example as dictated by channel policies about new target groups.

Fourthly, and probably most importantly, one cannot escape the fact that format is also used to describe a *commodity* circulating within the international television market for rights and intellectual property, for example at the MIP-TV and MIPCOM fairs held in Cannes, France (for descriptions, see for example, Moran and Keane 2006: 74ff). Furthermore, this commodity is the object of purchase and sale on a market that includes *both* commercial and non-commercial public service broadcasters.

In its capacity as a commodity, a format can also appear in different shapes. Firstly, we have *scripted formats*, such as television series or television drama (cf. Steemers 2004: 119). In this form, a format is equivalent to the remake within the film industry, in which a new version with new, local actors is made. The French film *Nikita* (1990) by Luc Besson, for example, was re-made in the US as *Point of No Return* (1993), in the same way and for the same reason the British television series *The Office* (2001) was remade with a similar script and dialogue as *The Office: An American Workplace* (2005) in the US. An interesting and widespread example of a successful scripted format is the Columbian telenovela *Yo soy Betty, la Fea*, which has been adapted to several national settings but also became a widespread series in its US form as *Ugly Betty*. It seems that this is a strategy frequently adopted in the US, where the general audience is not considered tolerant towards foreign films or television programmes, even if their origin is English or Australian. The cultural marker of 'Americanness' is also stressed in the title, in order for audiences not to mistake the copy for the original, probably on the same grounds that Mel Gibson's first Australian film, *Mad Max* (1979), was re-dubbed 'with American voices' when it was shown in the US (Maltin 1993: 777).

Secondly, there are *unscripted formats*, most often entertainment or light factual shows. The general idea behind an unscripted format (say *Survivor* or *Big Brother*) is a set of stable formulas and features that is written into the format 'bible', and which is the basis for its price on the television market. This bible often includes information on how to make the show and on budgets and scheduling, as well as more detailed information on how to select contestants, hosts, set design, the relation to the studio audience, etc. (Steemers 2004: 39). It can also comprise packages of advanced computer software, for example for the organisation of lottery draws, as in the case of Swedish *Bingolotto* (Bolin and Forsman 2002). The licence agreement of a format usually also includes consultancy services for setting up the programme in its new setting, and for the most part it is this service that is the real source of income for the company which has developed the format (Steemers 2004: 40). In many respects, however, the adaptation of the programme can be adjusted to national, cultural or other settings, or according to the premises and audience demands that are individual to each specific buyer of the format.

In this respect a format seems to be similar to copyright, that is, an economically-juridical agreement that secures for the holder of the right to an immaterial commodity the exclusive right to sell, distribute, lease or let out, etc., this commodity. A copyright, however, is only effective for a *work*, that is, a clearly definable text – a television programme, a song, a picture, a film, etc; It is the right to decide on the copies of this text. To be the legal owner of a format is similar in some respects. The owner of a symbolic commodity such as a format has the right to set a price on, sell, distribute, lease or let this commodity of his/hers. The crux is that the format commodity is not as easy to identify as is the individual text or work. As formats are sold on the basis of their success in one country, but are aimed at being adjusted textually for a new national or regional setting, they only comprise the right to capitalise on the concept, the idea of, for example, a television series. From this idea, an indefinite number of variations on this theme can then be produced in the form of television series such as *Big Brother*, *Survivor*, *Wife Swap*, *Supernanny*, etc. This naturally rationalises television production according to an economic logic whereby each production company specialises in a certain format (say, makeover shows), while other companies are better at other kinds of formats (say, mega charity events). Some formats have today also reached the scale of demanding trans-national cooperation in production, as is the case with the pan-European *Eurovision Song Contest*, which could be considered the most long-standing format in the history of European television, and also one of the few that has been developed by public service companies.

One could say that a format, in its capacity as an immaterial commodity aimed for circulation on a market, is more like a computer game than a book. As a printed medium, the book was the first to be regulated by copyright law. This was enacted for the first time by British Parliament in 1709 as 'the Statute of Anne', which afforded the author of a work 'the sole right and liberty of printing' for fourteen years (Kretschmer and Kawohl 2004). Music soon followed in 1777, but rights were not tried by law successfully by a composer until 1847, when after hearing his own songs played at the Paris café Ambassadeur, popular music composer Ernest Bourger refused to pay his bill with the argument 'You consume my music, I consume your beverages' (quoted in Wallis et al., 1999: 11). Although Bourger won the case, it was evident to him that he would never be able to control his compositions, since it was impossible to know every time someone used his music without compensating him. Unlike the book, whereby the basis for value generation is based on the 'physical distribution of tangible carriers' (Wallis et al. 1999: 7), songs are harder to control since they, if performed live, are more transient. If we then consider the format, which is also not laid down on a technical medium but mainly consists of ideas (a semiotic commodity), we realise that the valorisation process becomes even more complex. Furthermore, since the book is materialised on pages following one another, there is (at least most often) a linear narrative that structures the textual expression of the commodity. A computer game or a computer program, on the contrary, offers the buyer a conceptual world, for example the possibility to write a text like this, or to take part in a car race, football game, quiz show, etc., where the buyer can also play with others. One could say, then, that the need to regulate semiotic commodities arises with the increased possibilities for interaction with the text. When every single game on the computer is slightly different from the previous one, it is not possible to speak of the right to copy, since the possibility to make a copy presupposes an original work to make an identical copy of. An idea, as the principles for how a car race, football game, quiz show, etc., can be played do not permit the making of exact copies, but rather a series of variations within a given framework. In the same way, a television format can be said to function as a conceptual container that can be filled with a wide range of semiotic variations based on nationally and culturally specific particularities.

Not unexpectedly, it has proven hard to judge the limits of a format on judicial grounds, and locate the limits for infringement in the intellectual property rights of a format (Moran 1998: 15ff), although the industry has tried to solve this problem by launching the Format Recognition and Protection Association in

2000 (Waisbord 2004: 367). Although formats seem difficult to regulate they are accepted within the television industry, as most involved in the commerce with television programmes and formats accept the system of rights and licences, despite its weak legal framework. One could say that the system survives on grounds of a common belief that a format really is a commodity to be circulated within the field of television production, to use the language of Bourdieu (1977/1993). As long as there is a common belief in the value of formats, and a common interest to set a price on the format commodity, the system will remain. Seen this way, formats portray the audience as a symbolic commodity, constructed out of statistical estimations that are the regulatory mechanisms that set the price of commercial slots (Bolin 2005). Radio formats, argue Jody Berland (1990: 187), through their playlists offer 'a grammar of temporality which draws in the listener and *produces* her (economically, as a commodity; experientially, as a listener)'. In a similar vein, Australian media scholar Albert Moran argues that formats are only intelligible in their performative capacity:

> The term has meaning not so much because of what it is but because of what it permits or facilitates. A format is an economic and cultural technology of exchange that has meaning not because of a principle but because of a function or effect. (Moran 2004: 6)

It is clear from this quote that Moran does not consider formats in their technical aspect but rather emphasises their commercial potential, their ability to produce audiences as symbolic commodities that are then used by broadcasters for selling to advertisers. Indeed, his discussion on the meaning and character of formats opens up for perspectives that include both channel and programme formats, connected to their specific commercial workings within cultural production. That a television channel like MTV could be considered a format channel with a well-defined target audience does not rule out the fact that the channel can also broadcast programme formats bought from other producers. It might rather be the case that these two format principles go hand in hand in the production of the audience commodity within the television industry. The increased importance of scheduling, and the increased pressure on broadcasters to compete in a highly exposed situation, means that broadcasters are driven to continuously develop more well-defined audiences (as symbolic commodities) and convince their advertising customers that they are not paying for audience 'waste' (that is, segments of the audience that watch a show but that the advertiser has no use for and accordingly does not want to pay for; cf. Bolin 2002: 193). This is also why the television industry is so keen on continuously developing new rating systems that do not only present the audience commodity for one specific medium but can present this commodity in a more specialised way when it comes to media consumption behaviour. As BBC audience research controller Chris Mundy says in an interview, commenting on BBC's new web ratings system trying to capture 'cross-platform media' use:

The Holy Grail is trying to understand what each person consumes across the day, whether it is a podcast or listening to radio via TV. We want to know who is using new media and how much use is in addition to traditional consumption and how much is alternative. (*Broadcast*, 6 October 2006: 6)

Ironic as it may seem, this statement comes from a research unit within BBC, which does not have to package its audiences for advertisers. However, it seems as if highly professionalised (or perhaps standardised) production apparatuses develop their own internal logics, and that BBC is a player on a broadcasting field and needs to behave in line with other important powers that have influence on the field in question. This logic demands increased specialisation of programme distribution in order to further segment the audience for cultural-political purposes: Public service broadcasters need to account for their audience shares in order to meet political expectations in just the same way as commercial broadcasters need to meet economic expectations (for a more detailed discussion on this, see Bolin 2004b).

Although there are similarities between certain uses of the concepts of format and genre it also seems important to distinguish between the two, especially in relation to the format commodity. A genre cannot be commodified, either as a theoretical ideal or as a historical fact, since its principles depart from too-general conceptual characteristics (which are also in constant flux). A format, on the other hand, has at its root a well defined conceptual construction that makes up its core, the basic ingredient that cannot be changed (a family with untamable children, a group of people stranded on an island, a group of people locked inside a house, a specific type of game, etc.). For this reason formats are most often found within entertainment television, and perhaps most often in the reality genres (see Hill 2005, 2007). It is in fact quite hard to regard fictional series as formats, since fiction has the same features as novels of being 'works' with narrative closure, authors, directors, etc. Within narrative fiction you could produce a remake, something the film industry systematically does. You cannot make a remake of a format, since every national adaptation is in fact already a remake.

Formats, then, represent a way of nationalising or regionalising a certain type of content, in order to attract viewer interest, as viewer interest usually increases for national productions compared to international or foreign programmes (Straubhaar 1991, 2000: 199). As Annette Hill has shown, there is an explicit demand for national versions of internationally circulated reality shows, since, for example, Swedish viewers find especially US-produced shows to be 'sensationalist, overly commercial, and far removed from a Swedish mentality of "down-to-earth-ness"'. One Swedish viewer in Hill's study even asked: 'Couldn't they try to make a Swedish one, something produced in Sweden and something typical of Sweden, something that we can recognize ourselves in?' (Hill 2007: 219). This is also in line with what Silvio Waisbord (2004) has argued – that formats are shaped by the globalisation push of media economics, and 'the pull of local and national cultures' (p. 360). In their combination of structural similarity and local flavour, formats are, then, part of the process of cultural globalisation. Through format adaptations viewers in various national contexts are tied together by experiences of narrative forms that have the dialectic quality of having both a common international descent or provenance *and* a distinguishable national character.

This national-international dynamic also has counterparts in other media than television, media that also build on the engagement of their users. It can be noted, for example, that some of the most popular web services come in national variants. However much the web is transnational, even global, in its reach, there are national variants of Wikipedia (which might be understandable as some information will read best in a Swedish context, for example). But social networking sites such as Facebook, MySpace and YouTube also have their specific national variants. And for those that are not in national languages, such as Flickr, the content is nationalised – I get Swedish commercials when I log on from Sweden, irrespective of what language I choose in the menu. Arguably, these national variants are answers to the same problem that occupied filmmakers in the 1930s when they tried to address national viewers with films in national languages. The logic of cultural proximity carries with it that media users will prefer media content in their own language. This makes these attempts on the part of media producers similar over time, and connects them in their efforts to take advantage of rationalised media production, without losing the cultural specificities that literally speak to local media users in their own dialect. This was also the success formula that first made the bible popular (that is, spread among large numbers of people), with the technological advent of mechanical printing after Gutenberg, when it was translated and disseminated in vernacular languages. And we should note that this was also a consequence of new media technology.

In terms of media technology, format television takes advantage of digital technology, for example adding phone-in services or voting procedures to reality shows, or combining the content with extra material on the web, as is done in both news television production and entertainment as well as in print news media, where updates constantly change the news features so that they become a process rather than a fixed entity, which of course was the case in the print-only era. Hence we move into the area of multi-platform production. This will be the focus in the second part of the chapter.

Multi-platform Productions and Transmedia Storytelling

As indicated in the first chapter of this book, one of the consequences of digitisation is institutional integration and market convergence. Through 'tight diversification' (Rothenbuhler and Dimick 1982) media companies engaged in several media sectors try to take advantage of the narratives they have copyrighted, or through tie-ins, separate companies with similar interests join forces, such as when ISPs, search engine optimisers and advertisers jointly chase the digital consumer as described in Chapter 3. However, multi-platform productions not only integrate media organisations; they also open doors for innovative narrative constructions whereby different media technologies are drawn into the production process. Television is quite often at the centre of such formats, in which it is combined with other media, most notably the Internet and the web and the mobile phone, the radio and the press. These combinations take on many forms, one of which is 'transmedia storytelling' (Jenkins 2006, 2007), whereby several technological platforms are combined to construct greater narrative wholes than their separate parts.

In transmedia storytelling, media-content providers develop texts across several technological platforms, thus taking advantage of each platform's specific qualities and abilities. Transmedia storytelling, says Jenkins (2006: 21), is 'the art of world making'. The example he engages in is *The Matrix*. This science-fiction trilogy, he argues, cannot be fully understood from only the film text but needs to be complemented with the computer game. The story thus unfolds on several platforms, and was consciously produced to do so. This is how artists can develop narrative construction in more 'ambitious and challenging works' (Jenkins 2006: 96).

There are of course many examples that could be considered as early forms of transmedia storytelling in the form of 'remediated' narratives (Bolter and Grusin 1999), that is, narratives that have appeared on many different media platforms. Take the following example of a narrative that first appeared in a traditional medium (radio) and was then adapted to another traditional platform (a printed novel), to then become a computer game built on the original narrative from the radio play. *The Hitchhiker's Guide to the Galaxy* was first made for radio and broadcast on the BBC in the UK for the first time in 1978. The following year it was published as a book by the same author, Douglas Adams. The radio show was released as a recording and the radio production was also translated and produced for Swedish Radio, by the same translator who had translated the book into Swedish (Tomas Tidholm). In 1981 it was adapted for television, and in 1984 the narrative was released as a computer game (in English), in which you could follow the same adventure into space as you could in the radio play. The narrative of the game corresponded to the first book in the series, and it can be noted that Douglas Adams was also involved in the development of the computer game. Four sequels to the novel have since been published, and it was remade for film in 2005. It has also appeared as comic books, TV series, etc.

As I have shown in more detail elsewhere (Bolin 1994c), the narrative unfolding as well as the narrative complexity differ between the various media technologies in which they appear. As each media technology has its specific abilities when it comes to presentational possibilities, the narrative is a bit different. This is most apparent when playing the computer game, which indeed appears very simple in its gaming construction, judged against today's standards whereby sophisticated computer graphics and sound have become integrated parts of modern games. *The Hitchhiker's Guide to the Galaxy* computer game is based entirely on written text, and is indeed digital in its narrative construction in the aspect that each step of the game gives you two options, and depending on which you choose, the narrative will take a different route. The narrative progression is also of qualitatively different kinds. The first episode of the original BBC radio broadcast of 35 minutes corresponds to the first 51 pages of the first book in the series, and in the computer game we have reached step 35 and earned 25 points (of the total 400 possible points), given that we have managed to come this far in the game (which is in fact quite easy – it gets more complicated later). Already, by relating to the narrative progression in minutes, pages and steps, I have revealed something about the different qualities the narrative is equipped with in the various versions, which undeniably gives the media user a variety of experiences as it involves different senses. Experiencing a story with the same basic *fabula* (the overarching story), but whose *syuzhet* (the plot, that is, how the story is composed narratively) is constructed somewhat differently between media platforms, undeniably gives the reader a wider set of ways into the work, which should also expand on its textual universe.

The multi-platform production of *The Hitchhiker's Guide to the Galaxy* is an example of content production that has become more common because of the institutional integration and market convergence that privilege the spreading out of content over several platforms. This, however, does not mean that they are all examples of transmedia storytelling, as this specific phenomenon requires bits of the syuzhet to be spread out over several media platforms. The reasons for constructing transmediated stories can vary. As Yochai Benkler (2006: 4) has pointed out, information and cultural production has always been driven partly by non-market motivation, compared to 'traditional' industry (such as the steel industry, the car industry, etc.). Transmedia storytelling, then, has the dual quality of being both market and non-market motivated, or, to put it the other way around, it is driven by both artistic and non-artistic motivation. And transmedia stories can also result from the engagement of both the media industry (for economic reasons) and non-market motivated fans (for non-market reasons).

Stories, however, irrespective of whether they are produced for commercial or non-market reasons, are not only constructed in narration – a good part of how we understand stories has to do with what genre expectations we have. Post-structural genre theory has always included the context in the totality of expectations audiences have of films and television. As Steve Neale (1980, 1990) was among the first to acknowledge, we come to the cinema (in his case) with prefigured expectations drawn from reviews, advertising campaigns, word-of-mouth judgements, etc. If we extend this to the expectations of broadcast audiences, we can see today that many reality formats (*Idol*, *Survivor/Expedition Robinson*, *Big Brother*, *Bonde söker fru*, etc.) exist in symbiosis with the tabloid press, which is one kind of contextual component that influences audience expectations. When it comes to some contemporary texts, we can certainly see that the context is much wider than this, and that the line between text and context can be but analytically separated on pragmatic grounds.

That advertising campaigns, tabloid stories and other contextual environments can be included in the horizon of expectations that help audiences construct meaning from the broadcast event is not news to the updated researcher, of course, and it goes far back in the history of the cinema (fan magazines, etc.). However, if we think of the interconnections between broadcast reality and entertainment shows and the Internet, with mobile phone- and web-based voting procedures and other kinds of participatory elements, we could argue that this is a context of another kind. In fact, it could be argued that this is not context at all but rather an extension of the broadcast text, and thus a part of its generic construction. But where does this extension end? Does it include merchandise that surrounds some media works (for example, *Star Wars*)? New multi-platform productions provoke a new angle on the problematic, since some of the context today is also of a textual kind, just one click away on your laptop.

One way to try to distinguish between several types of textual expansion is to use Gerard Genette's (1997) concept of paratext, that is, those elements that are not normally considered part of the text but that 'surround' as well as 'extend' it. What Genette discussed were written works, thus the paratextual examples he gave were from books: 'an author's name, a title, a preface, illustrations' (p. 1). Genette discusses these as neither altogether outside the text nor inside it. He rather sees paratexts as 'thresholds' which guide the reader's interpretations. These paratexts are of two kinds: *peritexts*, which are 'the interstices of the text, such as chapter titles and certain notes', and *epitexts*, for example 'interviews, conversations', but also letters and diaries that can inform our reading but which are clearly outside the book (p. 5).

Being a literary scholar, Genette exclusively discussed books, and the distinction between peritexts and epitexts was very material to him: Peritexts were found inside the book whereas epitexts were outside it. Now, if we relate this to multiplatform productions and transmedia storytelling today, we can see that this distinction is harder to uphold. What is inside and outside a specific work in a world full of trailers, blog discussions, reviews, re-runs and spoilers is a much more complex question than what is inside and outside a book. Take a serial drama, for example, broadcast once a week. What would be the 'interstices' of the chapters of such a text?

Jonathan Gray (2010) usefully extends the discussion of paratextuality to the contemporary multiplatform media environment. With the help of Roland Barthes's (1971/1977) distinction between work and text – that is, between the more easily defined narrative, often with an identifiable author (director, composer) – and the text as the process that appears in the meeting between the work and an interpreting subject, he brings on the concept of paratext as a mediator between work and text, a contextual component to the work that can help widen the textual universe. The textual world of a certain book, film or play then extends to the relations between the individual works, their different paratexts and their audiences. In so doing, Gray makes an important distinction between 'entryway paratexts' and 'in medias res paratexts' (Gray 2010: 35ff). Entryway paratexts affect the reader's (viewer's, listener's) entrance into the text, with typical examples including advertisements, trailers and announcements, while *in medias res* paratexts are those textual elements that appear during or after viewing (reading, listening). These are the fan websites, the discussion forums, fan magazines, etc. In fact, Gray argues that 'much of the textuality that exists in the world is paratext-driven' (Gray 2010: 46). And indeed, it is perfectly possible to consume the paratexts and expand on the textual world without having consumed the work itself, as anyone who has read reviews of a film or record without actually having seen or heard the work in question could testify.

Roberta Pearson (2008) has also discussed the narrative aspects of transmedia storytelling across platforms in terms of paratexts. She has made a different kind of distinction than Gray has, between those paratextual features that directly contribute to narrative progression and paratextual features that *point to* the work, but contribute nothing or very little to the narrative progression within it.

These qualifications of the discussion, however, raise a problem for Jenkins's account of transmedia storytelling. If not all paratextual elements contribute to narrative progression, are they then not also disqualified from being components in transmedia *storytelling*? Stories and narratives are action-driven, and quite often, paratextual elements do not contribute to this (although they naturally contribute to the production of meaning in reception, for example by anchoring generic expectations). All stories have contexts, but not all contexts contribute to the causal unfolding of the narrative. As indicated above, the concept of transmedia storytelling is under-theorised in this respect. It does not distinguish between entryway and in medias res paratexts, or between paratexts that are important for narrative progression and what one could call 'pointers' to the narrative.

Two Cases of Transmedia Storytelling

There are two fairly recent Swedish examples of transmedia productions in which the television broadcast is extended to the web and mobile phone, representing two kinds of multiplatform productions. These are the entertainment series *The Truth About Marika* (Swedish original: *Sanningen om Marika*) on public service channel SVT2, and *Labyrint*, on commercial TV4, both broadcast (if this is indeed the right word) in the autumn of 2007. Surrounding these works is a range of entryway paratexts (announcements in schedules, interviews in tabloids before the premieres, etc.) and in medias res paratexts, albeit to various extents. As we shall see, the latter of these kinds of paratexts also had different impacts on the narrative progression of the two series.

Of the two, *Labyrint* is a rather traditional TV series and was broadcast once a week for twelve Thursday evenings at 21.00, beginning in October 2007. It extended to the web, where one could watch additional footage as well as comment on the episodes. It was also commented on in blogs. The basic plot revolves around a group of five young city people whose lives become intertwined through a series of events involving the running of the nightclub Blue and associated semi-legal activities. As the plot develops, the characters become more and more involved with each other, giving it all a plot structure comparable to *Magnolia* (1999) or

Table 5.1   Audience size for *The Truth About Marika* (2007)

	28 Oct	4 Nov	11 Nov	18 Nov	25 Nov
Fiction	350	210	200	165	170
Studio debate	240	210	135	120	105

Note: Figures represent thousands of viewers. The fictional part starts at 21.20, followed by a studio debate starting at 22.05. Figures from Mediemätning i Scandinavien (MMS).

Pulp Fiction (1994). The televised text was accompanied by extra footage on the web and 'mobisodes' on the mobile, in which extra information was planted. Very few blogs commented on this, and those that did pointed out that the information given was very obvious and was not needed in order to follow the narrative.[1] Judging from the few blogs that commented on this, it was not perceived of as important for the narrative. What was commented on more was the fact that TV4 changed the broadcast time from the prime time 21.00 to a later spot at 22.30 after the third episode, supposedly because it was not getting the size or composition of the audience TV4 wanted.

However, the extra narrative information on the web contributed very little to the overall understanding of the narrative, and was basically of a paratextual type that was unimportant for narrative progression; that is, information the viewer could easily do without and still find the broadcast television episodes meaningful. For TV4, the series was a major investment (production costs were 50 million SEK, roughly 5 million Euros), and it was expected to reach up to a million viewers per episode. The first episode, however, to the disappointment of TV4, 'only' attracted 726,000 viewers. The second episode attracted 399,000, and the third 282,000.[2] After the series was rescheduled to the later spot at 22.30, its audience further diminished to between 118,000 and 170,000, apart from the very last episode, which attracted 199,000 viewers.

The Truth About Marika was launched by Swedish Television (SVT) and was broadcast over five Sunday evenings (21.20) on SVT1 in the autumn of 2007. It was also fairly unsuccessful among viewers. Table 5.1 accounts for the audience statistics for the series.

Although the series did not meet with large numbers of viewers, it was more appreciated among critics and the media business itself, and the programme series was awarded an iEmmy for being the 'Best Interactive TV Service' of 2007.[3] This

---

1   See, for example, http://ragnevi.blogspot.com/2007_10_26_archive.html [Last accessed 11 June 2009].

2   All audience statistics are from MMS (www.mms.se).

3   Information about the iEmmy can be found at www.iemmys.tv/news_item. aspx?id=60 [Last accessed 20 December 2010]. A presentation of the series in English can be found on SVT's web page: http://www.svt.se/svt/road/Classic/shared/mediacenter/index.jsp?&d=71376 [Last accessed 29 September 2009].

'participation drama' combined broadcasting (in faked debate programmes as well as fictional episodes), the Internet (partly within the social world Entropia) and mobile services to create what SVT called 'fiction without limits'.[4] It is described as follows on SVTs web pages:[5]

> Marika disappears without a trace. When the case, after two years, reopens there is no evidence that she ever existed. 20,000 Swedish citizens have vanished and Marika is one of them. Why? What is the truth about Marika?

> The case of Marika draws attention right before the drama series premieres on TV. A young woman finds out that SVT is making a drama based on her blog, and she claims that everything is based on the disappearance of her best friend. SVT denies any part of this accusation and declare [sic] that the woman has made everything up, it's fiction. But the woman proves the contrary even though all traces have been erased. The case becomes a mystery.

> This is a "participation drama," created to enrich a drama production through the participation of viewers. The story takes place on television, the Internet, radio and mobile phones. Every week theories are discussed on a TV-show that in the end expose the truth about Marika. Viewers are directly involved in the plot and its conclusion. The mobile phone becomes an important tool in the twilight zone between fiction and reality, and bring [sic] the story to the streets into a fiction without limits.

The Truth About Marika played with several genres, including fiction, documentary and talk show, and was, in addition, also a live role-playing game with multiple layers of participation options. The viewers/participants were expected to engage in these options, which included the web site *Conspirare* (www.conspirare.se), as well as links to real-world criminal cases (for example, the murder of former Swedish Prime Minister Olof Palme and the resulting criminal investigation). It included blogs and chat rooms of both 'in-game' and 'off-game' types. Through the websites, participants were encouraged to take part in a fictional 'secret society' and contribute with photos and videos uploaded to Flickr and YouTube, and linked to *Conspirare*. It was also possible to submit content directly to SVT, which published some of it on its web site after editing, and included some of it in the (mock) debate programme that immediately followed the fiction/documentary episode. The programme text also included secret messages for viewers to discover.

---

4   All information about *The Truth About Marika* – unless stated otherwise – is taken from the official website of the show: http://svt.se/svt/jsp/Crosslink.jsp?d=73202 [Last accessed 29 September 2009].

5   http://www.svt.se/svt/jsp/Crosslink.jsp?d=81616&lid=puff_1007050&lpos=extra_0 [Last accessed 29 September 2009].

As can be understood from the above description, productions like *The Truth About Marika* clearly include features that are more than peripheral, that is, features that substantially contribute to the narrative's unfolding and progression. Hence, the production also raises questions about how we are to understand contemporary television works or media texts. Indeed, one could ask whether *The Truth About Marika* is one comprehensive work or programme, with particularly rich paratexts at its thresholds, or whether it is a combination of several works of different kinds and with different specific qualities: a live role-playing game, a television fiction programme, a fictionalised documentary, and so on? And, perhaps more important, if we were to conduct a textual analysis of it, which parts would we include in the analysis and which parts should we consider to be the context of the work? Which are the paratextual elements that point to the story told, and which are the components that contribute substantially to it (and in what ways)? We are faced here with a problem of interpretation to which there seems to be no straight answer.

Whether these are difficult or simple questions naturally depends on what you are aiming at. For the theoretically inclined media analyst an ocean of difficulties is opened, but for the audience rating system the solution was indeed easy. *Labyrint* is one television programme, and *The Truth About Marika* is two (the fiction story and the studio debate). At least this is how they are accounted for in the ratings system. This system does not take into consideration the various uses of mobile phones or web games and GPS services that were offered to media users – and naturally so, as the accounting system does not care about narration but rather penetration and segmentation.

In terms of textual analysis, however, one can indeed ask what the work is in relation to these two examples, and who the author of the work is. On the one hand, it is obvious that at least *The Truth About Marika* aimed at engaging viewers and users, and encouraged them to take part in the construction of the narrative. On the other hand, the contributions were not fed into the narrative automatically or unfiltered. In fact, as Marie Denward (2008) has shown in her study of the relationship between SVT and the co-producer The Company P, a production company specialising in alternate reality games, SVT did maintain strict control over the production and construction of the multiplatform story, which means that the opportunities for users to engage were quite circumscribed. As Denward suggests, this can in fact be one of the explanations for why the audience figures drastically decreased after the first episode.

The two examples given here thus represent two different kinds of transmediated stories. It is quite evident that the multiplatform production *The Truth About Marika* does include pieces that substantially contribute to the narrative progression of the work, including such contributions made by media users. It is equally obvious that the multiplatform production *Labyrint* could be understood perfectly well as a televised work, without the extra bits of information that were provided on the web. The information given might well contribute to the expansion of the textual world, but not to any narrative progression of the story. One could therefore indeed ask whether this is a case of transmedia storytelling.

It is quite clear, then, that not all multiplatform productions can be considered transmediated stories – not even all stories that are presented as fictional narratives. There are also a great number of multiplatform productions that do not aspire to be understood as fictional narratives, for example entertainment reality shows like *Idol*, *Paradise Hotel*, *Big Brother*, etc. It is therefore useful to clearly distinguish between transmedia storytelling and multiplatform media productions. Multiplatform production, then, is a way of organising content irrespective of presentational genre, to put together intelligently edited news, fictional stories, documentaries, etc. Transmedia storytelling, however, is more restricted than this, if we are to take the component of storytelling serious. Transmedia storytelling is about the composition of syuzhets that take advantage of the specific qualities and abilities of each individual media technology used, whereby technology at best is subsumed by the higher end of producing intriguing and entertaining narratives.

The Value of Multiplatform Transmedia Storytelling

As argued above, it is quite clear that not all the ingredients in multiplatform productions contribute to narrative progression, and it is important to distinguish, with Roberta Pearson, between those components that contribute explicitly to the narrative and those that admittedly contribute to the expansion of textual worlds but have very little or no consequences on the narrative progression. The latter phenomenon is hardly new, as the history of cultural criticism can testify. The criticism of musical events appears already in the late 18th century (Widestedt 2001), and literary criticism has an even longer history (although journalistic criticism appears around the same time as music criticism). In its evaluative capacity, criticism is also part of the formation of the fields of cultural production and consumption as theorised by Bourdieu, as accounted for in Chapter 2. Thus criticism, as a consecrating institution, is also engaged in the production of belief in the value at stake in the field.

One such consecrating institution is of course the iEmmy awards, handed out by the International Academy of Television Arts and Sciences, and announced at the MIPTV fair in Cannes. To underscore the importance of the prize, the Academy is presented as follows on their web pages:

> Founded in 1969, the International Academy of Television Arts and Sciences is the largest organization of global broadcasters, with members from nearly 70 countries and over 400 companies. The Academy was chartered with a mission to recognize excellence in television programming produced outside of the United States, and it presents the International Emmy® Award to programs in fifteen categories: Arts Programming; Best Performance by an Actor; Best Performance by an Actress; News; Children and Young People; Comedy;

Current Affairs; Documentary; Drama Series; Interactive Channel; Interactive Program; Interactive TV Service; Non-Scripted Entertainment; Telenovela and TV Movie/Mini-Series. (http://www.iemmys.tv/news_item.aspx?id=60, last accessed 21 December 2010)

The language of a presentation like this naturally has the function of imposing legitimacy on the prizes, and on the productions that have been nominated and awarded. Of course the iEmmy, a subdivision of the Emmy which has been awarded since 1969 (the iEmmy was institutionalised in 2006), does not have the same consecrating power as the Oscar, naturally a more prestigious prize, which can be ascribed to the fact that it is connected to the much older film industry, which through its star system and academic legitimacy is a much more powerful instance of conferring legitimacy. Nonetheless, the significance of there being an iEmmy awarded at all of course works within the subfields of television production and interactive gaming production. The Company P proudly relates to the iEmmy on their web pages together with a couple of other prizes representing 'International recognition for productions'.[6] In an interview with one of the founders of the company in a Swedish magazine, it is emphasised that the iEmmy helped the company get in contact with 20th Century Fox, leading to the production of a similar combined television series and interactive role-playing game called *Dollhouse/Dollplay* (the first season of which was broadcast in the US in spring 2009) (Löwenfeldt 2009).

The symbolic value acquired by The Company P through the iEmmy award might seem modest, and may be short-lived. The example, however, is not principally different from other kinds of productions. The value generated from the iEmmy might be weaker than the value an Oscar carries, and the consecrational force in this part of the field not very strong due to its clear placement in the unrestricted part of the field where the pressure from outer demand is higher. But since this part of the field is so dependent on outer demand (from the economic field of power in this case, or, as concerns public service television, from the political field of power), even weak consecrating instances will work in a legitimising way. However, irrespective of whether one acts in the field of restricted or un-restricted production, the principles for the accumulation of value are the same.

***

In this chapter I have discussed some of the new features of media content that result from institutional and market integration and multiplatform media production: the television format and transmedia storytelling. That television has had a prominent position in this chapter is by no means a coincidence. Despite all the talk about the death of television in the digital era, with users supposedly

6   http://www.thecompanyp.com/site/?page_id=233 [Last accessed 23 December 2010].

abandoning the medium in favour of the timeshifting possibilities of streamed content via some of the portals for television programmes or films – Voddler or blinkx, for example – television seems to have ended up in a stronger position. Television programme formats are often at the top of the hierarchy when it comes to multiplatform productions, whereas the web and the mobile are add-ons to the television programme. The reverse combination is rarer: Very seldom do we see multiplatform productions with the mobile or the web at their centre, with television as the add-on. The same goes for the other two traditional mass media, the press and the radio. Also here we can see that newspapers add moving images, sound clips and mobile phone services to their web editions, and have also been very quick to develop services in connection with the launch of the iPad. Radio, as well, as is the case with public service Swedish Radio, can add gaming components for children in addition to their children's programming.

Chapter 6
The Production and Consumption of Signs

In the previous chapters the changed role of media users in the culture industries has been discussed, as well as the changed character of works and texts which follow partly from new technological possibilities, partly from re-organisations of media production (which also, at least in part, are born from the technological changes), and partly from the described changes in the behaviour of media users. In this chapter I will bring these discussions together in order to more generally discuss the commodities and objects that circulate in the production-consumption circuits surrounding media. I will argue that there has been a profound re-shaping of the circulating commodities, from having been in the form of either texts or audiences to a situation in which these two commodities are changing in shape and form, and especially the audience commodity takes on a more semiotic character despite the widespread belief from within the industries that we now have better tools for 'grasping the digital consumer' (see Chapter 3). This discussion will involve a thorough critique of the circuit of media production, from its basis in tangible commodities (or content specifically bound to specific material platforms) to the intangible commodities and ephemeral objects circulating in the digital media and cultural environment.

In his critique of Adorno's (1941) cultural industry perspective on popular music, Bernard Gendron (1986) argues that there is a profound difference between traditional industrial production and production in the culture industry (he refers to it in the singular), which at the bottom line has to do with the specific quality of the commodities produced. Gendron's main argument is that, for all the merits of Adorno's position, Adorno is also 'misled by his industrial model' (p. 30), making him assume that 'the conditions which require industrial standardization in the culture industry are similar to those which require it in the rest of capitalist industry' (p. 26). This leads Gendron to distinguish between 'functional objects' produced by, for example, the car industry, and 'textual objects', produced by the culture industries.

Gendron makes this distinction in order to capture some of the consequences of cultural production, as opposed to traditional industrial production. His terminology – functional as opposed to textual objects – is, however, somewhat misleading as it implies that textual objects cannot be functional. Of course they can. Texts from the culture industries can, for example, have quite physical effects (if we speak of effects in a broader sense than in the media effects tradition). They can have the function of mood management, as when we construct or arrange a social encounter, say, the first date with someone we are attracted to, by playing something we feel is appropriate as background music. Or, as Linda Williams (1995) has shown, different film genres obviously have a functional side to them, such as melodrama, horror or pornography, which are all genres that have specific functions relating to the phenomenology of the body – to touch us emotionally, to make us frightened or sexually aroused. Or, as I have analysed at greater length elsewhere, music and visual media can help regulate and adjust the flow of customers in shopping malls and other public spaces (Bolin 2004a). When used in this way, music and visuals become cultural technologies whereby cultural expressions are used for other ends than for producing cultural value. In the case of shopping malls, then, mediated cultural expressions become means for the production of economic value. Or, put in another way, cultural expressions are consumed in the process of producing exchange value.

Equally problematic is the distinction made by Scott Lash and John Urry (1994: 15) into two types of sign commodities: those with 'primarily cognitive content' and those with 'primarily aesthetic' content, the latter being what they call 'postmodern goods'. This distinction is problematic, as it supposes that content is formless (pure information) and aesthetics are without any informational dimension (pure form), and seems to reproduce a naïve apprehension of what art is and how information is packaged, and it is hard to see how this crude distinction could be of help.

The conceptualisations of the digital, sign-based commodities are many, and in Chapter 1, I commented on the division between material and immaterial commodities, a distinction that is often made but that is also misleading, since digital commodities also have material qualities (and indeed leave their very material remains in the form of electronic waste and greenhouse gas emissions – which could possibly be called intangible waste). Light flowing through fibre optic cables has an undeniable physical materiality, which according to the laws of physics can be transformed into other forms of energy. Sound waves in the air also have their own materiality, and hit our eardrums in quite manifest and physical ways. Sound, by definition, cannot be put in our pockets. It is intangible, but nonetheless material. As argued previously, then, it is more appropriate to distinguish between intangible and tangible objects.

Intangibility, the evanescent character that marks contemporary digital objects, is in fact not exclusively confined to digital objects and commodities. Several analogue media contents that preceded digitisation have the same intangible quality. Television programmes and radio broadcasts are examples of such intangibles, as Thomas Streeter (1996) has pointed out. But digitisation undeniably brings with it a change in character with these analogue media contents as well, and again I would like to stress the historical parallel of the shift to digital reproduction with the Benjaminian shift to mechanical reproduction that I have accounted for. In the same way as Benjamin analysed what happened to the work of art in the age of mechanical reproduction, there is a need to account for the consequences on cultural objects that occur with digital reproduction.

In the first section of this chapter I will more thoroughly discuss the specific character and construction of intangible objects and commodities as combinations of signs, and highlight their specificities as compared with tangible commodities. In a second section I will relate these objects and commodities to the fields of production and consumption, pointing especially to the consequences digitisation has on the circulation of these. This includes relating the sign commodity and its role in fields of signification to the regulative frameworks of the digital economy. In this section I will focus especially on four kinds of sign objects and commodities: media content, media audiences, the traffic commodity, and brands. In the third section I will sum up the discussion in an argument about the belief structures that need to surround sign commodities in order for them to have value.

Sign Commodities

Arguably, and as pointed out by Gendron, Hesmondhalgh, Benkler and others, the commodities circulating in media and culture production have some specific qualities that distinguish them from non-cultural commodities. To Gendron (1986), Adorno's fallacy was mistaking the part interchangeability that was effective in, for example, the car industry, with that in cultural production: Each car of a specific brand can change individual parts with another car of the same brand without problem and function well. This is not valid for music. You cannot take the chorus of one hit song and exchange it with the chorus of any other hit song, as this will result in a new commodity (a mash-up, for example). Hesmondhalgh (2007) stresses the fact that cultural artefacts are not worn down in use to the contrary of most other industrially produced goods, and to Benkler (2006), cultural production is driven by non-profit motives to a much higher degree than other kinds of production are: It would most certainly be unthinkable for the informant referred to in Chapter 4 to work with 'crap' eight hours a day for free, while he was perfectly willing to work long hours writing fanzines, and later producing avatars for the multiplayer computer game Quake 3, without pay.

All these distinctions are naturally valid for describing the specific character of cultural objects and commodities. But they are not sufficient. The specificities of cultural objects are also radicalised in the digital era, as many of them have no tangible base but are pure sign structures, a fact that also provokes a distinction between tangible and intangible cultural objects and commodities, which I call sign commodities here. Admittedly, cultural objects have always had an intangible character. A piece of music, for example, is hard to put in your pocket or hold in your hand, as is a performance at the theatre, a recited poem, an enlightening lecture, a radio play – at least when it comes to the *performance* of all of these examples. If laid down on tangible carriers – the printed scores or a recording of a performance of Beethoven's *Symphony no. 9*, the printed play *The Tempest* by Shakespeare, the recording of a performance of *Howl* by Allen Ginsburg, the printed inaugural lecture *L'ordre du discours* by Michel Foucault, the LP recording of *The Hitchhiker's Guide to the Galaxy* – they naturally can be held in our hands, which up to the point of digitisation was the most common way for us to experience these works. With digitisation, however, we no longer need these tangible carriers as we can reach all these works on the web. This is the radical difference between analogue and digital circulation of cultural objects.

This means that the political economy of the intangible cultural commodity also differs from that of the tangible cultural commodity. As has often been pointed out (for example, Murdock 2000: 55f), Marx did not live to see the rise of modern mass media and of the 'information society', in which manifest and tangible commodities have increasingly been replaced by intangible, semiotic commodities. Although there are occasional references to symbolic production, for example the production of knowledge (Marx 1867/1976: 644), this is no point on which he elaborates, and he quite naturally could not foresee the consequences of the shift to 'informational capitalism' (Castells 1996). This fact, it can be argued, does not only affect his relation to commodities as manifest and tangible entities, but it has also led him and others to underestimate the symbolic character of the economy. In Marx's theory, economic capital is quantifiable and possible to estimate and count in objective terms. Capital is subject to mathematical laws. In the elaboration of the theory of value, Baudrillard admittedly expands on this theory to develop a political economy of the sign. Although he acknowledges that 'the epicenter of the contemporary system is no longer the process of material production' (Baudrillard 1973/1975: 130), he has surprisingly little to say about the opposite, the 'immaterial' or intangible commodities that he argues have become dominant. In fact, it can be argued that Baudrillard was slightly ahead of his time when he theorised sign value, and although he struggled hard to understand the changing modes of capitalism he was still caught in the idea of the commodity as having some material (tangible) base to which sign value became attached. This is also how one can explain why his writings are not entirely coherent, for example when it comes to distinguishing the *tangible* commodity with sign value from the *intangible* commodity with sign value, a distinction I argue is at the heart of the shift we are presently involved in.

A typical example in which Baudrillard (1968: 83f) explains the importance of the sign for commodity exchange (and for the game of social difference) is how we are no longer buying functional commodities but rather the signs attached to them. American cars were long appreciated for their extravagant tail fins, obviously connoting 'flight' or 'speed'. As Baudrillard argues, this is the triumph of the sign over function. We do not buy the function of 'speed' (in fact, the tail fin makes the car heavier and clumsier). What we buy is the sign of speed, the sign that connotes 'that is certainly a powerful, fast car'. And what we achieve with the consumption of this purchased commodity is the difference we are ascribed by others: 'He/she really drives a fast car'.

This example concerns a quite traditional industrial commodity – the car – that has been designed in a way that enhances its price on the market, and in this, the sign components contribute to its exchange value. This phenomenon, as I have indicated in Chapter 1, was already observed by Galbraith (1958/1964), who discussed how advertising problematised traditional economic theory.

Table 6.1   Relationships between value, sign and form for tangible objects

use value	signified	object form
exchange value	signifier	commodity form

Baudrillard's interest does seem to lie in discussing the similarities between use and exchange value and the components of the sign, that is, signifier and signified. He argues that there is a structural similarity between three pairs of concepts relating to value, sign and form: use/exchange value, signified/signifier, and object/commodity form.

This set of relationships needs to be discussed firstly in relation to tangible commodities and, secondly, in relation to sign commodities. If we adopt the example of a Volkswagen car for the tangible commodity, we can define its use value as the costs of the general labour needed to produce the car, plus the costs for the raw material. As the car has a manifest and tangible 'object form', it is also easy to recognise its status as signified (that is, the mental conception of a Volkswagen car). When we see the signifier 'VW' or 'Volkswagen' in a text such as this, for example, this mental conception arises – the object form springs to mind on account of the activation of the signifier. The exchange value (the value that springs from the commodity form) is defined as the price the car has on the market. Exchange value thus relates to use value (the object form) in the same way as signifier to signified. The relative arbitrariness of the exchange value to the use value is structurally similar to the arbitrariness between the signifier and its mental conception, the signified.

If we look at a sign commodity instead, say a piece of music, the relationships change somewhat. A jazz tune naturally has a use value, although this value does not consist of raw material in the same way as a car does. However, it is certainly the product of labour. And it obviously has exchange value: Its copyrights could be sold, or it could circulate on the market to people who appreciate jazz music. We could also say it could appear in object form and not only commodity form. The jazz tune could be played by an amateur with no intention to record or distribute it on other occasions besides live performances (which are not aimed at producing surplus value). It would then have object form but not commodity form. Or it could be produced within the music industry for commercial reasons. Whatever the case, the structural similarities are short-circuited if we try to analyse the signified of the tune. At the level of commodity (or product, for non-commercial objects) there exists no signified; only a signifier. This signifier is, then, pointing to itself: The signified of *Mack the Knife* is the same as its signifier, *Mack the Knife*. There are naturally several signifieds that are provoked by the signifiers *in* the tune – the lyrics consist of references to knives, sharks, teeth, etc., all of which provoke mental conceptions. But *the song as a commodity* has no signified. 'The signifier/signified distinction is erased', as Baudrillard (1976/1993: 87) puts it (but in relation to another pure sign commodity: fashion). Its specific composition of sounds does not refer to any other mental conception than that of this specific composition. (The concert performance of *Mack the Knife* by, say, Ella Fitzgerald, should not be confused with the sign commodity as distributed to listeners. The commodity at a concert is the performance of the tune, and not – at least not only – the tune as aural sign.)

However, this fact only counts for those sign commodities that are circulated within a 'pure' sign system. A reproduction of the painting the Mona Lisa, for example, is different in this respect. The sign 'Mona Lisa', irrespective of being two names put together as in this text, or in a photographic reproduction, has a signified: the mental conception of the actual painting by Leonardo da Vinci that we can see, and many obviously have seen, at the Louvre in Paris.

An objection to this argument could be that most consumers actually *have* a conception of an 'original' version of the song. When we hear the tune *Yesterday* in a Muzak arrangement at a department store our mental conception might be of the original Beatles recording, or of Paul McCartney as the singer or composer. From the perspective of the production-consumption circuit, however, this does not matter. Paul McCartney is no more the signified of the sign *Yesterday* than Leonardo da Vinci is the signified of the Mona Lisa. There is, admittedly, an intertextual connection, but this connection has very little to do with the process of value accumulation in the economic field of production (although it might be of importance for the production of social difference in another field).

Another peculiar feature when it comes to 'pure' sign commodities lies in the very act of consumption. For a material commodity, the use value is destroyed in consumption (a car is ultimately so worn down that it cannot be further used or circulated on the market). This is not the case when it comes to sign commodities, as David Hesmondhalgh (2007: 21) and with him many others, argue in relation to CDs and DVDs. However, a CD could break, the plastic dry up and wear out, etc. But if we imagine the jazz tune as a composition of signs (digits) possible to download from the Internet, this is not so. The main point here is that sign commodities in the age of digital distribution and circulation on the internet are increasingly freed from tangible form (as opposed to being stored on a CD, LP, DVD, etc.). Furthermore, the absence of tangible features for the sign commodity makes the system more reliant on the *means of consumption*, as has been pointed out. You cannot listen to a jazz tune that is freed from object form unless you own a radio, a computer, an iPod. And as the means of consumption, at least within the sphere of music consumption, are being exchanged at increasing speeds, consumers are led to purchase and consume the same sign commodity over and over again, albeit adjusted to ever-new means of consumption (first the LP record, then the CD, then the MD, then the iTunes song).

There is also another aspect in which Hesmondhalgh (and others) are not entirely right when describing the characteristics of the cultural sign commodity. What is implied when one says that 'cultural commodities are rarely destroyed in use' (p. 21) is that they are eternal. And in a way, one could say that digital sign commodities have the *potential* of being eternal, even if this capacity of the commodity is in fact seldom realised. Thus the use value of intangible commodities cannot be destroyed in consumption in the same way as that of material commodities can, by being worn down through use. Sign commodities can only be destroyed or *consumed by other signs*. And this is indeed a peculiar feature of sign commodities. They have the potential for eternal life, but this also makes them problematic from the production-consumption perspective. If all cultural commodities were eternal, we could reach the point of satisfaction as consumers, content with the number of tunes we have access to, the number of films at our disposal, or the number of texts we can download to read.

Take fashion as a phenomenon. If we were content with the clothes we own, and they satisfied our needs for warmth and shelter from the sun, and are functional to work or rest in, why would we need more clothes? How could anyone produce surplus value from clothes, if fashion did not contribute to the exchange value by adding sign value. And as sign value is realised in consumption, the consumer of fashion will mark him- or herself out as different. Fashion is typically described as an example that builds on 'aesthetic innovation', as argued by Wolfgang Haug (1971/1986: 39ff). This refers to the process by which a producer, by 'periodically redesigning a commodity's appearance ... reduces the use-lifetime of the specific commodity' and thereby subordinates its 'use-value to brand-name' (p. 40f). It is naturally easy to find examples of such redesign strategies in the present. The advertising campaign by Apple when launching the iPhone 4, already mentioned in Chapter 2 – 'This changes everything. Again' – is one such example. Even more striking is the update between the iPhone 3 and the iPhone 3GS. The latter is an identical gadget visually, with a few new functions (most notably the ability to record video clips). It is thus not an aesthetic but a technological innovation. Since its introduction on the market in early 2007, iPhone has (at the time of writing) arrived in four generations, which means that the early adopters have had to upgrade once a year.

Haug, however, never really explains how aesthetic innovation happens (only *that* it happens), why the new becomes more attractive to consumers, and what consequences this has on the production-consumption circuit. To understand this we need to acknowledge that the function of the sign value encapsulated as a possibility in the new commodity is *to destroy sign value*. At the moment of destruction, with the attack of the new sign commodity on the old through the release of next year's fashion (the next pop music icon, the next film star, the next iPhone model) last year's creations become realised and we enter into a new circuit of signification. This new circuit is related to the old one by being different, thus producing new sign value (the consumption of which produces social difference in the field of consumption). Furthermore, the destruction by fashion of the sign value in the consumption process is not by the hand of consumers but rather of producers (thus making it productive consumption if viewed from within the field of consumption). The destruction of value becomes an effect of the system, which then becomes self-generating. What we face when it comes to fashion is the self-sufficient system; fashion as *auto-consumption*. We are faced with signs consuming other signs.

When the sign value of the new commodity destroys that of the old one this also affects the exchange value, making the second-hand value of commodities substantially lower, on par with the use value (as equal to the cost of production), and sometimes even lower. Sign value does not age well, and for tangible commodities this has profound consequences. The new sign commodity becomes attractive to consumers not because it is new, but because the old has become waste, useless as a distinctive marker in the field of consumption.

It should be noted that fashion in clothing is a hybrid in that it indeed has a tangible base (cloth, linen). One should also acknowledge that although this argument might hold for all kinds of fashion, it is more obvious if one looks at haute couture. All fashion is marked by its sign value and functioning but there is a continuum, with the mainstream design of H&M at one end and haute couture's Dior, Yves Saint Laurent or Givenchy at the other. Haute couture is naturally a more instructive example at the high end of the continuum, as these are clothes that are designed in a way that no one expects them to be worn except for the sake of producing difference – at grand openings, gala premieres, royal weddings, etc. In this capacity, haute couture is (almost) a pure sign commodity, but the general principle of sign value is also valid for the mainstream design of H&M. Haute couture, then, escapes use value in the same way as money, 'the first "commodity" to assume the status of sign', as Baudrillard (1976/1993: 22) points out.

The destruction of sign value in circuits of commercial production means that the sign component continuously works to devour (destroy by consumption) the exchange value of the commodity on the market, and continuously seeks to destroy its distinctive power in other fields, for example that of cultural production. This cannibalistic quality of the sign commodity also explains the reappearance of previous features in cultural production – the retro fashion, the constant return to previous genres and sounds in film and music, the pastiches made – and also accounts for the homage paid to earlier directors, composers, etc. This is the devoured sign reappearing; not in any identical way but rather slightly transformed as if it had not been digested properly. This is the stylistic signs of 1950s youth culture reappearing in *American Graffiti* (1973), the 1970s aesthetics of blaxploitation recycled with a twist in *Jackie Brown* (1996), or the aural signs of the 1990s resurrected in Robyn's *Dancing On My Own* (2010). It has less to do with the individual biographies of the authors of these works than with the collective experiences of generations: the generation with which George Lucas grew up in the 1950s, the one Quentin Tarantino spent his youth watching *Shaft* (1971) and similar films together with, and the one that, along with Robyn, danced to synthesised disco beats in the 1990s. It is the signs devoured then that, from the pile of waste produced at that temporal moment, are drawn into the future, establishing them as 'the past's presence' (cf. Schuback and Ruin 2006).

This continuous presence of the past in each seemingly novel cultural phenomenon adds a circular, or perhaps more accurately, spiral character to production in culture and media industries, as the past does not just repeat itself, as Marx (1852/1971: 33) put it, either as tragedy or as farce, but as reminiscence – of signs having other signs as signifieds. In the next section the consequences of this on the processes in fields of production and consumption will be discussed in more detail.

Fields of Signification: Restriction and Dispossession

How are the fields where these sign commodities and objects circulate constructed? And what kinds of value are produced in them? Although Baudrillard expands and develops Marx's theory on the production-consumption circuit, it is far from clear how this affects the everyday production and consumption of signs and material commodities. It is evident, however, that he seeks an explanation for how value is produced (and which kinds) that transgresses those laid out by Marx. As concluded in Chapter 2, we have to turn to Bourdieu to find a discussion on the production of other kinds of symbolic value (or capital, as Bourdieu insistently calls it). He also has little to say about media production, but the advantage of the field theory is that it makes it possible to account for how different kinds of symbolic capital (including economic) can relate to one another in the distribution and production of difference related to social life. However, although it is easy to see the Marxian influences in Bourdieu's theory (as it is in Baudrillard's), it is also important to mark out the major differences. One of these is the view on value, or capital. If Marx sees (economic) exchange value as an objective entity, Bourdieu sees it as an *objectifiable* entity, in the sense that it can be objectified *in relation* to other values, although not objectively measured in any way. Bourdieu, then, stresses the relational character of a value, and how it develops or transforms over time (and under the hands of labour and the structures of the field of which it is a part). But, like Baudrillard, Bourdieu emphasises the symbolic or non-material features of commodities, their ability to function as distinctive when consumed. And even more importantly, Bourdieu provides us with a tool for understanding how symbolic capital (economic, social, cultural) is generated as an effect of the relationship between the structures of the field, and of the agent's actions.

The basis of Bourdieu's theory is that value is produced as an effect of the relationship between agents and institutions in a social field, based in the struggle between these agents and institutions over a value, or capital that is considered worth striving for. The value is simultaneously produced as a result of this struggle. In Marxist terms, one could say that the activity of struggling is the labour that produces the value. This value is specific to each field, which has its own institutions for evaluation and consecration. In a field of production – the art field, to take Bourdieu's main example – there are consecrating instances (art critics, museums, art journals, etc.), positions (acknowledged artists, curators, etc.) and a value (art). In a field of consumption, the struggle is for social differentiation, the value being prestige, influence, charismatic leadership and general, social recognition.

The sign commodity can be related to the fields of both production and consumption. It is important to be aware that even if these are similar they are not identical, and while the principles of valuation are the same and evaluations in fields of consumption have consequences on the field of production, there is no automatic correspondence. This is because producers and consumers do not always strive for the same values. The principles of value accumulation are also the same, however, and work irrespective of whether it is *the field of cultural production* (where cultural and aesthetic value is produced), *the field of the economy* (where economic value is produced), *the political field* (where the value produced is political power), or the *field of knowledge or academic production* (the value being knowledge, understanding, and academic legitimacy).

We can illustrate the relations between the fields of economy and culture by momentarily returning to the earlier example of the Bentley and the Toyota. As I tried to show in this example, the sign value of the Bentley contributed to the exchange value of the car as a commodity. However, as it was also stated that the sign value helped to produce difference between me and my workmates we need to acknowledge that this difference is produced *in another field* than the one in which economic exchange value is produced. Just as economic profit is the result of the ability of the owners of the means of production to take advantage of the economic profit, the cultural profit at the centre of the field where difference is produced results from the ability to make *a differential profit* by way of consumption – it distinguishes me from my co-workers in their eyes, and also in the eyes of possible observers. Differential profit can be achieved in two ways: either by consuming quantitatively (having a multitude of cars, hundreds of shoes, etc.), or qualitatively (consuming only highly refined culturally prestigious commodities, for example, legitimate art). And in a structurally similar way to the logic of the field of production, it is more effective to produce difference through qualitative than quantitative consumption. One Bentley amounts to a higher sign value than four Toyotas; One extravagant dress from Alexander McQueen, John Galliano or Vivienne Westwood outweighs four dresses from H&M or Gap. This is highly different from how economic value acts. Economic value does not have quality, but only quantity. More beats less. A hundred thousand Euros beats fifty thousand. Not even the different currencies will make any qualitative difference, as there are conversion rates that create commensurable and exchangeable quantities. Ten US dollars, depending on the conversion rate at a specific point in time, will have an exact exchange value in relation to other currencies, irrespective of whether it has the object form of ten one-dollar bills or one ten-dollar bill. The amount of paper will not make any difference. It also will not make any difference if you have a ten-Euro bill or ten one-Euro coins.

An important difference between exchange and sign value, then, is that sign value cannot be quantified and accumulated in the same way as economic exchange value can. The symbolic value of the sign does not have the additive quality of economic value. This is all the more true for pure sign commodities such as content, audiences, traffic, and brands. None of these were born with digitisation, but even as they all precede this process they have been altered by it, changed in fundamental ways. They are not the only commodities circulating, but are central and important to the fields of cultural production and consumption, and in the next few paragraphs I shall account for how they have become altered and the consequences this has had on their circulation.

Sign Commodity I: Content

In Chapter 1, I referred to Thomas Streeter's (1996) observation that television content is an early form of intangible production. Television programmes are undeniably intangible (as are audiences as statistical aggregates), and circulate both in fields of cultural production either as end products in themselves or – within commercial production – as the means to construct the audience commodity. However, before the video recorder appeared, media users had very little power over this content, and had no possibilities to share or manipulate it. With video recorders this changed, and with digitisation one can say that television content has been freed from its earlier forms as it is now possible to record, manipulate and disseminate it outside the control of its original producers.

The same goes for many other kinds of media content that were intangible in the analogue era: radio broadcasts, music (both of which became possible for media users to access with tape recording technology), and the cinema (when it became accessible on video and later DVD). With the increased possibilities for users to access, manipulate and disseminate media content outside the control of the media industries, rights questions and digital rights management (DRM) came to be of crucial importance, whereby questions of piracy and illegal file-sharing moved to the top of the agenda for the media industries (Burkart and McCourt 2006). In this sense, digitisation only radicalises processes that started in analogue media production and consumption environments. As I showed in Chapter 3, this dramatically changed the ways these industries organised themselves, and how they have increasingly moved towards what the industries call customer-relationship management (CRM), in the words of Patrick Burkart and Tom McCourt a system 'intended to build and track audiences', while digital rights management 'is designed to regulate their online activities' through a range of sophisticated technological solutions (Burkart and McCourt 2006: 101).

However, although some parts of the media industries are changing their business models this does not mean media content is set entirely free for anyone to use. In fact, with digitalisation an immanent contradiction has developed in the media and culture industries, provoked by the fact that media users increasingly contribute to the content they consume. It is in fact highly important for media producers, be they broadcasters, social networking sites or web-based news media, to retain the rights to the content they use to attract audiences and create the audience commodity, as this is the basis for how their end products are produced. You cannot consume raw material in production if you do not first own that material. If you are to build a house, you need to buy the material with which it is to be built. If you make cars you cannot combine the parts if you do not first own them. You do not steal the material when you build the house, nor do you rob someone of interchangeable car parts for the one you want to build. In principle, the same is valid for intangible production. So, media producers need to secure ownership of all raw materials used in the production process, and media content is such a component. This is why intellectual property rights will remain important for the media industries for the foreseeable future.

I wrote 'in principle' when I indicated the similarity between tangible and intangible production in the previous paragraph because, as I argue, in the wake of digitisation the conditions for how raw material is appropriated have indeed changed. With digitisation, much of the content consumed by media users (who are the basis for the calculations of the audience commodity) is actually produced by the media users themselves. This is especially true for social networking sites such as Facebook, Flickr, MySpace, YouTube, Twitter, etc. But the industry is very careful not to allow these 'produsers' the right to their own content. In the words of Peter Jakobsson and Fredrik Stiernstedt (2010), this is a form of 'primitive accumulation', by which the media and culture industries 'through a process of *dispossession*' rob the people who labour for free not only of their work, but also of the results of that work. This form of 'state-sponsored piracy' means that social networking sites (Facebook, MySpace) and search engines (Google) 'extract' the values produced by the labour of users. So while the media industries carefully patrol the borders of their intellectual property rights, they simultaneously disregard the property rights of the 'produsers' who work within the limits of the industries' communicative structures.

The ingenuity of social networking sites is their double function as generators of value in both the field of production, where they produce exchange value by selling their users to advertisers (and, presumably, to anyone who wants to buy them) and the field of consumption, where they help produce social difference for consumers (or possibly, prosumers). From the fact that they dispossess their users of the result of their labour, however, it does not follow that they want to sell the content they produce to others. The aim is rather to use the user-generated content as raw material to produce the commodity sold to advertisers. And this fact makes this type of production different from that of the house or the car in the examples above, as you cannot industrially produce commodities on the basis of stolen raw material.

This is indeed a dramatic change in the premises for media and cultural production, as it extends the sphere of production to areas previously outside the market through 'primitive accumulation'. Primitive accumulation is the term Marx (1867/1976: 873ff) used to describe the initial basis where capital was formed before it went into circulation and was reinvested in order to produce more capital. As Marx describes it, it is 'an accumulation that is not the result of the capitalist mode of production but its departure' (p. 873). To Marx this only happened once, when the commons became enclosed and land that was previously free to use became private property.

Many have taken up Marx's idea about primitive accumulation and brought it into the digital economy and Web 2.0, mostly from the perspective that intellectual property in the common domain is appropriated and copyrighted, preventing the general public from using it freely (for example, Boyle 2003, Hemmungs Wirtén 2008). Such primitive accumulation, however, is far from new in media industries, and one need only think about Disney's accumulation of tales and stories from the cultural commons. This accumulation, argues Lawrence Lessig, is not problematic in itself. Rather, he says, this is a sort of 'creativity that we should remember and celebrate' (Lessig 2004: 24). The problem arises when the accumulating party, for example Disney, locks down and prevents others from using what was previously in the common domain. As Lessig argues, the present legislation has secured that 'no one can do to the Disney Corporation what Disney did to the Brothers Grimm' (Lessig 2003: 764). At least not before the year 2023, when the extension of Disney's copyright expires, although many suspect that Disney will lobby for another extension (Hemmungs Wirtén 2008: 121f).[1]

In a slightly different way, Jakobsson and Stiernstedt (2010) argue that this 'accumulation by dispossession', as they term it in line with David Harvey's (2003: 137ff) update of Marx's model, extends to wider areas of Web 2.0. In the present digital environments, argue Jakobsson and Stiernstedt (2010), 'we (users of the Internet) are, in the informational economy, given the means to freely express ourselves, communicate, and form relationships outside of the structures of the traditional cultural industries'. In parallel to the dialectics of freedom/ exploitation that Marx analyses at the break between feudal and capitalist society, according to Jakobsson and Stiernstedt the flip-side to the freedom provided in the Web 2.0 setting is that 'participation goes from being restricted and privileged to becoming mandatory'. In a similar way as Baudrillard and Bauman have argued that consumption today has become a duty rather than a pleasure or a right, this accumulation is not of objects previously accessible to all, but of our own lifeworlds. This brings us back to the discussion in Chapter 4 about audiences and labour.

Sign Commodity II: Audiences

Chapter 4 contains a description of the two active audiences theorised in media and communications research. The first of these is the active audience of political economy, regarded as working for the media (television). The second is the active audience of cultural studies, producing meaning, identity and culture from interpretive work in relation to media texts. These two theoretical constructs have today merged into the media user in the Web 2.0 setting, who actively contributes

---

1   Copyright protection was prolonged from 50 to 70 years after the death of the author through the extension granted by the US congress, enacting the Sonny Bono Copyright Term Extension Act (CTEA). The extension was provoked by the fact that Disney's Mickey Mouse was about to fall into public domain (Hemmungs Wirtén 2008: 121).

to the circulation of content through file-sharing and uploads of pictures, status markers, geo-social positioning information, etc. on social networking sites and search engines. According to the terms of use on these sites, for those who read these very long and detailed documents, they do not privilege the rights of the user-generator, who is instead dispossessed of the contents he or she produces, as described above.

Activity is a value embraced by all interested parties in media production and consumption, and one that has been emphasised in active audience theory. Activity, however, does not equal power, nor does being active lead to powerful positions (although the absence of action surely leads to its opposite). The advertising business also wants audiences to be actively engaged in the commercial messages (and to help distribute them through viral marketing on YouTube, for example). Activity as a value, then, is uncontroversial. No one would want media users to be passive.

The very character of activity, however, is the focus of debate. When Jhally and Livant (1986) argue that the television viewers are working for the networks by producing 'surplus watching time', it is very hard to see how the surplus value is estimated. We do not know exactly how many people in the audience are actually watching (or listening, or reading), but they are the prey of those who produce this information: the marketing divisions at the media companies and their consultants. When it comes to the production of wooden chairs, we can know quite precisely how much wood and how many work hours it has taken to make a certain number of chairs. We can, if allowed, enter the factory and examine the raw material as well as watch the labour process. We thus have a material base for our calculations. But how is this calculated within sign production, regarding things like the statistical composition of the audience?

The circulation of the audience commodity on the media market depends on the willing suspension of disbelief among the agents in this field of production. As Thomas Streeter (1996) observed, those involved in media production care surprisingly little about the poor quality of audience ratings. Everyone involved in media production knows that audience statistics are not the same thing as the 'real' viewers; that they are an estimation of how many people are watching, based on the activities of the circa 1,200 people with people meters in their homes (to take the Swedish example). However, it is equally known that it is impossible, or at least too expensive, to adopt methods that would give exact figures for the whole population. If we were to enter this factory, we would definitely be able to meet the workers, if I am allowed to continue the analogy of the factory, but there would be no raw material to be found. The exchange value of the commodity, then, is highly dependent on the silent agreement on the fact that this commodity, which is actually entirely dependent on the sign status of its object, is good enough to come to an agreement on a price (exchange value).

In the field of cultural production media content is less and less considered a commodity in itself, and is rather regarded as raw material in the productive consumption of the audience commodity. Coupled with this gradual shift, executives in the business are also openly acknowledging the constructed and negotiated character of the audience commodity. Both commercial and public service broadcasters acknowledge the need to 'agree on a common currency'.[2] This 'currency' is, for both commercial and public service broadcasters, the audience ratings. This does not make content unimportant, however, as it is content that helps produce the ratings. Some content is better at producing this commodity than other content, especially if it is combined with a specific time slot. Programmes, especially programme series, have this function of helping construct a good audience commodity – many of these are format productions, but some are also fiction and sport. It is not always a matter of the programmes that attract large audience ratings, although a format production like *Strictly Come Dancing* obviously does in all the countries that have adopted this format. It can just as well be a programme with a well-defined target group. And sometimes these two features coincide.

Although the terminology of 'currency' stems from the economic field of power, it is translated by public service broadcasters into values that supposedly work towards the political field of power. You could say that the concept of 'currency' means something else in the public service setting than in the commercial environment. It is translated into the value form that is effectively working in the political field, giving legitimacy to the programming policies of public service broadcasters. In order to be invested with this other value form it needs to be semiotically filled with other signs, connoting other beliefs than those that govern the economic field. So, if the commercial television production demand on the audience commodity is that it be narrowly restricted to the target segment in terms of age, sex and education, the valued audience in the public service production environment could be composed to fulfil some of the public values that this part of the field of television production embraces: a broad, inclusive audience, or one that addresses groups with no commercial value, such as the elderly (those over the age of 55, for example), ethnic minorities that are of no interest to advertisers, etc.

While money is the acknowledged value form in the field of the economy, there is no corresponding measure in the field of cultural production, no exact way to define social, political, cultural or aesthetic worth. The use of the concept of currency should be regarded as an attempt to produce a common belief that there in fact exists a measure within the media and culture industries. This is a fetishisation of the audience commodity by abstraction, an objectification into a value form that is quite far removed from the conceptualisation of television viewers as working for the broadcasters (labour), an administrative logic reducing human activity to the initial capitalist sign commodity: money.

----

2   Quote from Carl Hemmingsson, Chief Marketing Officer of Swedish TV4. Personal communication, 5 May 2009.

Sign Commodity III: Traffic

That media users are active and have the power of agency is, as argued above, not controversial. It is a value embraced by all kinds of media producers, and by different strands of media research alike. That media users are active is, however, not only a rhetorical pose in contemporary media 2.0 environments. It is in fact a requirement. If audiences in the pre-digital era were accounted for as aggregated consumer profiles along sociological variables, this is not enough in contemporary media environments. Media users are required to actively contribute through the uploading of documents, or the production of electronic traces on the web.

Telephone service, as argued in Chapter 3, was an early form of business model that was built on user-generated content. The telephone companies provided users with the means of communication, in order for them to engage in conversation with friends, relatives, business contacts, etc. This service was appreciated by its users, and the telephone companies were able to profit from providing this service by charging fees. The same goes for the postal service: People found it useful, and were prepared to pay to create content that was communicated to distant others. As long as people made calls and sent mail, the companies cared little about the content of those letters and calls. And although it was possible for the switchboard operators to eavesdrop on calls, this was not done systematically and turned into a business model.

In the digital era, the information about which calls are made (and which applications are used) is not only charged for through a fee per megabytes used, but is simultaneously sold as information to advertisers. We can call this the commodification of consumption: Our consuming of the service of using the telephone or Internet is turned into a commodity in itself, extending the area subsumed under the commercial logic of capitalist production. With this we move from the production of the *general traffic commodity* to the production of the *specific traffic commodity:* the combination of signs produced in consumption. As a sign commodity, the specific traffic commodity is far more complex in its composition than is the general traffic commodity. As the specific traffic commodity is constructed from a wider variety of signs, the possibilities for manipulation and aggregation into lifestyle patterns based on movements on the web increase, and with this increase follows an equivalent increase in its economic value on the market where intelligence about traffic behaviour is bought and sold.

Sign Commodity IV: Brands

In the traditional industrial production of tangible commodities, brand differentiation is adopted as a strategy to separate one commodity from another within the same functional area. With increased market competition, branding strategies become more important, and hence the sign value of commodities, as the value brands are built on, seemingly takes command over the functional use values of objects and commodities, and the sign value itself becomes the most important object of consumption (Baudrillard 1968: 229ff). We need only take a quick look at the mobile phone market to realise that brand recognition is more important than the technological information of functionality, and through their (de)sign strategies Apple has been particularly successful, creating hype around their products, most notably the iPhone and iPad. Through this, a strong consumer demand is created, built less on functionality and more on sign appearance: When the iPhone 4 was launched in the Nordic countries, test panels in technical magazines voiced strong criticism of its functionality, the web journal Slate even terming the product 'iSorry'.[3] This did not prevent customers from pre-ordering the gadget, however, and the mobile phone providers Telenor and Tele2, who sold the iPhone 4 in the Nordic countries, obviously used this to fuel the hype.[4]

The intangible qualities invested in sign value naturally need to be protected if it is to be turned into exchange value for Apple and others whose commodities build strongly and sometimes even entirely on (de)sign components. We thus have legislation regulating trademarks, design, patents, copyright and other intellectual rights, as well as passing-off, unfair competition, etc., all of which are designed to protect the property of the media and culture industries (Humphreys, 2011). For intangible commodities in digital form, which have the technological quality of being easily distributed and endlessly reproducible, copyright and similar rights are of fundamental importance as it is only through copyright that one can simulate the restrictions that form the basis for there being a market for the product. Use values of things that everyone has access to, such as the air we breathe, 'virgin soil, natural meadows, unplanted forests' (Marx 1867/1976: 131), cannot be turned into commodity form without the restrictions produced through incorporating the object within intellectual property rights. The labour that produces these values as commodities, then, is the labour necessary to turn it into exchange value (cf. Elson 1979).

Such restrictions, however, are not at all as effective in the digital era as one would suspect. Restrictions on the market cannot really explain why the iPhone has a higher sign value than its competitors produced by Nokia, Ericson or HTC, who all shamelessly copy design features from their main competitor on the market. It needs to be acknowledged that Apple in their (de)sign work succeeds in loading its products with aesthetic values that give them a competitive advantage, and this is the work of make-believe – not make-believe as in false, but as in *seductive* or *making others believe in the sign components*. Sign values do not just appear out of nowhere; They are produced through signifying practices. Behind their possible success lie many hours of sign work – not immaterial work, as some

3 'Steve Jobs Owes Us an Apology. What the Apple CEO should do about the iPhone 4's antenna woes', *Slate* 15 July 2010, http://www.slate.com/id/2260465/ [Last accessed 24 January 2011].

4 'Lång kö till nya Iphone trots den hårda kritiken' (Long queue for new iPhone despite criticism), *DN.se* 31 July 2010, http://www.dn.se/ekonomi/lang-ko-till-nya-iphone-trots-den-harda-kritiken-1.1143012 [Last accessed 31 July 2010].

have conceptualised it (Hardt 2005; Lazzarato 1996), since this work is indeed experienced as intense and concrete for those who engage in it (see examples in Deuze 2007), but symbolic work as in 'working with symbolic construction'. However, this is not only the symbolic work of producing distinct design forms. It is equally the symbolic work of producing *belief.*

Universes of Belief

In fields of production and consumption, as Pierre Bourdieu (1977/1993) has insisted, the ultimate result of production (and consumption) is the *belief* in the value produced. This value can be economic, but it can also be of other kinds: cultural, political, social. If we refer to the example of the audience commodity in the commercial economy, it can be argued that what advertisers buy from television stations (or other producers of audiences, such as commercial newspapers, radio stations, weeklies, etc.), is not the actual viewing time of actual existing subjects, but the belief in the statistics accounting for, or rather representing the idea of, a number of social subjects within a certain age span, and with a certain lifestyle profile (cf. Meehan 1984) – an imaginary audience, or a sign commodity, if you wish. Exactly how this is constructed might be exemplified in the following quote:

> 'We are very proud to provide media organisations and marketers across Sweden with a webTV currency they can trust and use to allocate their marketing budgets most effectively', says Gerben Boot, General Manager Nedstat Scandinavia. 'We will measure all video streams including live and the complete viewing experience. This will give accurate numbers for all programs, large and small. Also we are already prepared to combine these absolute numbers with demographic data for detailed target group information'. (Web Analytics Association 2010)[5]

As the quote reveals, the audience is constructed with the aid of the new measuring technique adopted for measuring the watching of web television, through making the customers of the international web analytics company Nedstat Scandinavia 'trust' that the figures presented are 'accurate' and 'absolute' with reference to 'demographic data' for the target group of one's choice. Trust is then one of the most important ingredients in the production of belief.

The audience commodity is, in fact, a perfect example of how sign value not only contributes to the exchange value of immaterial commodities, but actually *is* the commodity, and how a belief in the sign 'the audience' is upholding the system of production in late modern, industries of immaterial production. The audience

---

5   http://www.webanalyticsassociation.org/news/43059/Vendor-MMS-selects-Nedstat-for-webTV-measurement.htm [Last accessed 21 January 2011].

as a sign commodity is such a signifier without a signified: It is a commodity that lacks an external referent, as well as any signified outside its own sign system. The signifier 'the audience' points to the constructed statistical measure 'the audience'. At the point at which the statistical measure is acknowledged as a construct that does not correspond to any social fact, it also becomes a commodity bought and sold at a price set by the belief system of the media market.

The same goes for the television format as a sign commodity: As there are weak legislative frameworks that prevent competitors from stealing the ideas that are efficient in the market for audience production through format broadcasting, there has to be a strong and mutual trust in one's competitors. This has been explained by the double-bind that broadcasting institutions and productions companies are tied up in, where one day you are the seller of a format, and the other a buyer (Humphreys 2011). In such acts, the market for sign commodities is constituted.

This trust and the belief produced in the television markets are, however, a bit different from the market for user-generated content on social networking sites and search engines. Arguably, this is a sector of the media and culture industries that are producing new commons that they then can approach and engage in accumulation by dispossession. This has become one of the defining features of the Web 2.0, and this way of producing value is somewhat different from the practices in the television industry. The ingenuity of the social networking and search business is the observation by Jakobsson and Steirnstedt that, unlike the primitive accumulation of land that Marx discussed, the accumulation by dispossession that takes place in the digital environment both robs media users of the fruits of their work and simultaneously provides them with the joys of that work – presumably the joys that make the users continue to up-load and place their work and content at the disposal of the media and cultural industries. With user-generated content, a body of content appears that is seemingly free for all to use, and in this respect it constitutes a cultural commons. This commons attracts users who engage in the production and consumption of content, resulting in their constantly being dispossessed. This form of perpetual accumulation by dispossession, whereby the media industry invents new commons that can then be appropriated through accumulation by dispossession, is indeed parallel to the boar Sæhrímnir in Nordic mythology as described in *The Prose Edda* by Snorri Sturluson, who was consumed by the Viking gods each night at Valhalla but each morning arose anew for perpetual consumption.[6] With this, we also reach a state at which new production of value is based on the productive consumption of consumption.

---

6   *The Prose Edda* can be found on the web, for example in the Internet Sacred Text Archive: http://www.sacred-texts.com/neu/pre/index.htm [Last accessed 31 January].

Chapter 7
Digital Markets and Value

What does it mean to say we value a thing? What is the basis for our judgement? Raymond Williams (1976: 87) once famously stated that the word culture was 'one of the two or three most complicated words in the English language'. He later lamented in an interview: 'I've wished that I had never heard of the damned word. I have become more aware of its difficulties, not less, as I have gone on' (Williams 1979: 154). I do not wish to say that this is equal to my experience, nor do I wish to suggest that I am on a level with Williams in terms of sophistication in my cultural analysis, but by analogy one could say that the concept of value is equally complicated in its wide variety of uses and in its plurality of connotations. Quite naturally I have not exhausted its varied meanings, and there is certainly much more to say in terms of analysis of the position of value in culture and society.

Value, as I have argued throughout the book, appears in many different forms and results from a variety of processes. It is not one entity, unified and homogenous, although as discussed in relation to the media and culture industries it is most often connected to the sphere of economics. As I hope I have shown in the course of the preceding chapters, the uses of the concept need to be broadened, not for its own sake but because a delimited use of the word also delimits our appreciation of the wide variety of phenomena with their own special logics for value accumulation and their own autonomous status as fields of production or consumption in their own right: art, knowledge, politics, etc.

At the same time it can be concluded that it is very hard to escape the economic dimension when value is discussed. How can this be explained? Why is it that economic worth has such permeating power over other value forms? Why is it that we always slip back into economic metaphors, and to economic conceptualisations of things that are clearly outside the market? It would be very easy, and indeed tempting, to blame this on neo-liberal discourses and their dominant place in contemporary debates, but that would be altogether too easy an explanation. And anyway, it would only further lead to the question of why the neo-liberal discourse is so dominant. Others have engaged in this discussion more systematically (for example, Couldry 2010), and I will not add to the debate in this context (although I will briefly return to Couldry's argument about voice as value in the last section of this chapter). What I would like to do instead is focus not on economic value, at least not *per se*, but on the dynamic *relationship* between aesthetic, social and cultural value – and how these are positioned against the market.

In this last chapter, then, I will start by summarising some of the main trends and features I have discussed in more detail in the preceding chapters. In a second section I will return to the field model presented in Chapter 2, and with its help will try to make some conclusions about the dynamics of the fields of cultural production and consumption and the power tensions that structure these fields. Another way to put it is that the first section concerns the empirical conclusions while the second accounts for the theoretical conclusions.

Production and Consumption and Digital Culture Industries

The preceding four chapters have all dealt with production and consumption, although each from a slightly different perspective and with different emphasis on the varied instances involved in media and culture industries. Chapter 3 focussed on production contexts, organisational forms and business models, mainly from the vantage point of the industries. Chapter 4 switched focus from the structures of the industries to the consumption practices of media users, as well as the labour users are involved in, and had a special focus on the changed conditions for media use and engagement in digital environments. In Chapter 5 media content as works and texts was discussed; first the increasing spread of format television production, and second the multiplatform content and transmedia storytelling that extend far beyond mass media content. Chapter 6 focussed on the specificities of sign objects and commodities, and the radical reconfiguration of the sign object in digital informational capitalism.

In the continuous analysis of media and culture production over these chapters, I have attempted to apply a dialectical perspective that accounts for the dual nature of digital media production and consumption. Much media theory has adopted an either-or position, either taking its departure from the dominance of the media industries which exploit media workers and take advantage of media audiences, or taking the active audience perspective which in its extreme form celebrates each and every sign of engagement with media content on fan sites or Facebook. It has been my sincere wish to reach beyond such positions in order to develop a more nuanced understanding of the dynamics and interplay in the relationship between media use and media production. This means adopting, firstly, a perspective that phenomenologically seeks to understand the values activated in media use and consumption and then, secondly, from a more structural vantage point analyses how these values are exploited and turned into exchange values in media production. However, it also involves the analysis of how media use and consumption produce social difference through the consumption of sign value. This phenomenon, I argue, can be understood if we think of it as two separate, but indeed interrelated, fields. The first of these is the field of cultural production and the second is its corresponding field of consumption.

The Dialectics of Production and Consumption

The production-consumption dialectic is but one of the features I have repeatedly returned to in the preceding chapters. One area of concern when it comes to the creation of value is the ways media and culture production is organised, and the frameworks in which production takes place. Due to digitisation, as I have argued, the media and culture industries have had to re-organise, developing new business models that build less on content delivery and more on service provision. In fact, the combination of providing revenue-generating services to users, with the selling of these users and their behaviour to third parties, has arisen as a new opportunity in the digital era – an option that media industries did not really have in analogue times. In Chapter 3 the mass debates of earlier periods in media and communications history were set in relation to thoughts on the mass personalisation of the present, and in an extension of this argument one can reflect on the fact that although the traditional mass media have increasingly turned to niche audiences (albeit still built around sociological variables), the new digital media and the business models connected to them build on the aggregation of media user data on an even larger scale. If business models are to take advantage of the 'long tail' philosophy of media marketing (Anderson 2006), it is of utmost importance that the figures from which one targets consumer behaviour are large enough to make this philosophy profitable. As the commodities at the end of the tail will attract quite few, it is imperative that the market actually spans most parts of the world, or at least enough potential consumers. This is also why companies like Google strive for maximum access to the raw material that is the basis for the audience and user commodity. When Google bought YouTube for 1.65 billion US dollars, what they bought was the consumption force of the users of YouTube (although their rhetoric says the merger 'will create new opportunities for users and content owners').[1] And what they are trying to achieve with Google Books is to monopolise the world readership's consuming power.

That new, technologically founded business models are available does not always mean that they will be adopted full-scale. There is ample evidence, most notably also in the older media industries, that there are tenacious structures and culturally deeply rooted practices that are making what could be revolutionary changes more outstretched in time. To return to the example of how the television advertising industry developed new ways of administrating audiences through new models for advertising placement (RBS or 'run-by-station'), this has not yet meant that all advertisers take advantage of these more effective means of constructing the audience.[2] This is most likely also true for business models formed around purely digital content. Perhaps this is also beneficial for a system in which

---

1 Google, press release from 9 October 2006, http://www.google.com/intl/en/press/pressrel/google_youtube.html [Last accessed 30 January 2011].

2 This is also the logic of cultural tenaciousness that makes the niche channels of TV4, for example, economically less successful than anticipated. Although TV4 runs almost 30 niche channels, it is the main channel that brings in most of its revenues. Advertisers put their ads on the broader mainstream channel rather than on the niche channels, according to Göran Ellung, Head of Factual Programming at TV4. Personal communication, 28 January 2011.

'stagnation equals regression', as the discourse in the industry goes: If the system is not optimised, there is still space left for expansion and increased profitability.[3]

And this expansion builds on the administration of consumption and the continuous construction of new markets. Production is not the problem in late digital capitalism, at least not the major obstacle for increased turnover. Production has the technological means – including the social technologies of organising production – to solve most possible problems. The most pressing problem is the administration of consumption.

Social and Digital Consumers

With digitisation the digital consumer also surfaces as sign commodity, freed from any social referent. Mobile phones might be considered a personal medium, but as a generator of the traffic commodity or as part of cloud capitalism, it matters less who you are in terms of sociological variables such as age, sex, education or marital status, and more *where* your digital presence is and whether you are mobile enough to be accessible to location-based advertising and traffic. User traffic is the commodity – not the social mobile user, but rather the user's activities on the web. What counts for the media and culture industries is presence and movement in digital space rather than status in social space. And with the further estrangement of the digital self from the social self – which is triggered by the need of the companies that build their business models on crawling the Internet to persuade their users that their social selves are *not* being surveilled, that they indeed *retain* the right to their own uploads, and that privacy *is* taken into consideration – the pure sign stands out as the object circulating in economic or social space.

So, it is not your social self but your customer persona that is addressed. Furthermore, in digital culture it is unimportant whether people lie and give incorrect details about themselves on their personal blogs, their Facebook pages or any other social networking site. Lying about your age, sex or ethnicity is unimportant. It does not matter, as what is bought and sold is not your personal but rather your digital self, and the economic system will be quite healthy even if the data are not true, as in correct concerning social reality. It becomes a self-generating belief system founded on the sign commodity, freed from the social referent. As long as all involved parties believe in the intangible sign commodity, the system will work. The request for users' acceptance of the terms of use and their promise to 'provide their real names and information, and we [that is, Facebook] need your help to keep it that way' is a message to Facebook's customers – those to whom the users are sold as an aggregated digital commodity. Whether users submit to this and other terms – such as not having more than one account and keeping their 'contact information accurate and up-to-date' – will not really matter in the end, as

_____

3   Quote from then Managing Director Thorbjörn Larsson in TV4's 1998 Annual Report.

long as advertisers and other Facebook customers believe in the commodity.[4] And it is this belief that is the basis for the economic value to Facebook and the field of cultural production, just as it is the basis for the social and other values produced for users. Users will also need to believe that who they are communicating with are the actual people behind the profiles.

If the role of the consumer has changed from the social self consuming goods against the background of his or her sociological features (sex, age, socio-economic status, etc.) to the digital self drifting about in digital space, the character of the media user has also come to spend his or her time in a new digital context. In an eloquent, although not entirely unproblematic, discussion in his book *Remix*, Lawrence Lessig (2008) argues that the 'read/only' culture, born with the printing press and sustained through analogue culture over books, newspapers, magazines, film, television, radio, etc., is but a parenthesis in media history.[5] In this parenthesis, culture has become locked in by being tied to a tangible carrier, having become a commodity circulating among consumers who have had no ability to manipulate or in any other way co-create dialogically with the cultural expression. If culture before the advent of the age of mechanical reproduction (admittedly a term Lessig does not use) was 'read/write', or co-creative, by nature, culture has since been the object of consumption for the vast majority. Pre-mechanical culture meant singing, dancing, reading, etc., together in co-creative settings. Each and every person who wanted to could partake in cultural creation. The read/only culture, by contrast, was only for consumption. Today, with the widespread access to the means of cultural production, ordinary citizens can again join in the production of culture. We are again entering a read/write culture.

There is, of course, something accurate about this account, although one can also argue that Lessig plays down the co-creative opportunities that actually have existed in what he calls the read/only culture. And as I have tried to describe in Chapter 4, media users have always been active, and have also been theorised as having agency. Agency, however, has appeared in many shapes (that is, valued in various ways), and has contributed to the creation of value in many different ways (and in several different value forms). If we think of the value forms produced in cultural production, it is also obvious that what Lessig considers a parenthesis (in my analysis of his account, that is; he uses a different terminology), is actually a re-appearance of *some* traits of the age of non-mechanical reproduction. Lessig's account is linear (just as the parenthesis is a temporary abruption of a sentence, after which the sentence continues in linear progression). To me this is not a parenthesis, because there is a lack of continuity. It is a historical moment that has affinities with another *point* in time, producing a connection *through* time, to another past,

---

4   Facebook Terms of use. Available at http://www.facebook.com/#!/terms.php [Last accessed 31 January 2011].

5   Lessig (2008: 28) borrows the 'read/only' and 'read/write' terminology from the permissions attached to computer files. Read/write permissions allows the user to manipulate the file, read/only files can only be read.

connecting with *some* features of that past while also adding some. It is digital rather than analogue time. Analogue time is continuous, like water. Digital time is punctual, like separate moments occurring in a repetitive movement around the clock, re-connecting previous moments, re-constructing previous pasts.

As mentioned, however, Lessig is not entirely wrong. Something has changed with the advent of digitisation: The means of consumption have indeed also turned into means of production, whereby ordinary media users can be creative in content production. This production is often non-market-oriented, and although the media industries do dispossess the media 'produsers' of the results of their labour, in circulation, these objects are consumed by other media users, producing sign value. From the vantage point of these users, aesthetic, social and cultural value is produced in signification.

With organisational and technological convergence the media and culture industries are in conjunction with *parts* of the media users (as far from all media users accept the offer to contribute to digital content) involved in the creation of increasingly complex media works and texts. Co-creation itself produces social value (belonging, self-esteem, etc.), but there are also aesthetic and cultural values produced in the collective signifying practices, as I have shown in the previous chapters.

In line with classical critical theory in the wake of the Frankfurt School, we could indeed ask the foundational question: 'Whose interests are served by media users being drawn into production in this way?' In terms of value, there are at least two answers to this question: It serves the media and culture industries, who make (often huge) economic profit, but it also is appreciated by consumers (prosumers, produsers) engaging in these practices. This is the true dialectic that Horkheimer and Adorno (1947/1994: 167) referred to in their culture industry essay when they held that 'consumers feel compelled to buy and use [the culture industry's] products even though they see through them'. By analogy, digital consumers/producers today often know they are targeted by the media and culture industries, but upon reflection find this cost bearable. But, what is more, the young Facebook user who has all his or her friends on this social networking platform has very little choice but to join the digital community. Resisting being present in digital space *also* comes with a cost, a cost that for most young people would seem unbearable. It would be digital homelessness.

The Sign Commodity and the Market for Signification

In the preceding chapters I have discussed several types of sign objects and commodities: audiences, formats, various kinds of media content and works of both professional and amateur natures, etc. Sign objects and commodities are typically intangible, and the most obvious of these also precede digitisation: Broadcast television programmes, music on the radio, theatrical performances, cinema experiences, etc. In the read/only era, as Lessig (2008) terms it, these were difficult to manipulate by their users (although the spectrum of interpretations could produce a wide variety of texts, in Roland Barthes' [1971/1977] conceptualisation). With digitisation, those works that were previously bound to their tangible forms have also become 'liberated', and have thus also become increasingly transient in character.

As I discussed in Chapter 5, other intangible sign commodities also circulate in the media and culture industries. The format is such an intangible commodity, with extremely weak legal frameworks, but nonetheless appears as a commodity that is bought and sold. This can be explained by the belief produced in the field of television production in this very commodity. In fact, it is the belief itself that produces the format as a commodity. If the agents involved in the television industry did not believe in the format as a commodity it simply would not be one, and no one would consider paying for adapting it to a new national setting. Through the common belief in the format as a benefit for the television market, the object becomes a commodity. This specific belief in the format as a commodity was constructed first in the 1990s. Previously, national broadcasters launched national versions of programmes that had been successful abroad without the slightest thought of paying for the right to do so. The legendary American quiz show *The 64,000 Dollar Question* from the mid-1950s (1955-1958) was unashamedly adopted in Sweden as *Kvitt eller dubbelt* (1957-1961), also popularly called 'Tiotusenkronorsfrågan', as the prize sum was 10,000 SEK.[6] At that time, the belief in formats as a commodity was yet to be formed, and hence the format did not have any exchange value on the television market.

Another commodity produced by the media and culture industries is the audience commodity, a typical product of the traditional mass media, connected to the audience-based business model. It appears with broadcast media, although it is prefigured in connection with the press. With audience ratings, this commodity is produced through the signifying practices of statisticians and marketing managers. Initially it was based on sociological variables (sex, age, income, etc.), but has more recently been freed from its social references and turned into profiled digital behaviour. With the change from analogue to digital media, this commodity becomes increasingly signified, that is, it becomes increasingly estranged and removed from the social subjects it is supposed to represent. Through this it becomes the ultimate sign commodity, as it receives autonomous status in reference to its referent: The social subjects that watch, listen and read the content that the mass and personal media provide them with. With new features such as geo-social

---

6   Just like its US original, the Swedish version was immensely popular. The most famous contestant, and the first to win, was then 14-year-old Ulf Hannerz, who later became a world-renowned anthropologist (see for example, Hannerz 1992; 2004). Hannerz was first judged as giving the wrong answer, but was reinstated and received the prize sum of 10,000 SEK. Principles of digital rights management (DRM) will prevent this link from being accessed from outside Sweden, but those with access can see Hannerz win at http://svtplay.se/v/1370923/oppet_arkiv/1957-02-09__10.000-kronorsfragan_-_kvitt_eller_dubb elt__1_14_?sb,k103243,1,f,103244 [Last accessed 31 January 2011].

positioning, this commodity becomes more connected to the communication technologies (iPhones and other smartphones) than to the social subjects that are the targets of the commercial messages. However strange it might seem that 'geo-social' positioning is gradually having less to do with social subjects, this is a kind of 'technification' of the commodity, making it increasingly abstract and technological. This market for the audience commodity also builds on belief (as indeed any market does, as John Kenneth Galbraith [1970] observed early on) – in this case the belief in technology providing accurate information about positions, behaviour, etc. Almost needless to say, markets based on belief are very sensitive. In a way all markets are based on belief, but markets for pure sign commodities can easily be modified and sometimes also destroyed in signification.

Web-based technologies naturally also provide users with the means to share and disseminate self-produced media content on a scale previously not possible. The amount of user-generated (and user-distributed media industries') content is increasing by the minute. This means that the sphere of digital content is continuously increasing, growing larger and larger every day. With this comes an increased area to exploit through data-mining and appropriation by dispossession, and one way to think of it is as the solution to the problem of capitalist production and the limits to exploitable material resources. If land was 'the decisive factor of production' until the mid-18th century when capital began replacing it, as John Kenneth Galbraith (1969: 356) argues, one could propose that the decisive factor of production in the age of digital reproduction is computational control over digital space. For Marx (1867/1976: 873ff), land was the object of 'primitive accumulation' at the break between feudal and capitalist society. Land, as a material and highly tangible entity, has its limits. It is not endless. When all land is under ownership, other 'decisive factors' need to be invented. My suggestion is this: What if all the expansion of user-generated production, that is, the production that results in things outside the commercial market, in the end is just an effect of the market logic to find continuously new areas to expropriate as markets? What if Wikipedia and other crowdsourced and open-access production were invented in order to make them able to be intruded by market forces at a later stage?

Value in Fields of Cultural Production and Consumption

A common misconception about Bourdieu's field theory, mainly in its English reception and perhaps much in connection with his work on cultural consumption in *Distinction* (1979/1989), is that he unmasks the social mechanisms by which taste is used for social domination and that he is opposed to art, aesthetic judgement, etc. What is noticed less is his insistence on the autonomy of the field of cultural production (including journalism), and the value of upholding this autonomy and seeing to it that the field is not contaminated by other value forms (mainly economic, but there is of course always the risk of political intrusion and attempts at taking over the value forms produced in fields of cultural production).

An oft-repeated claim in Bourdieu's work is that the field of cultural production is increasingly threatened by the 'world of money' (for example, Bourdieu 1992/1996: 344), no matter whether this concerns the cultural production of television and journalism or the production of art and consecrated culture (cf. Bourdieu 1996/1998). Unfortunately, he never discusses this in relation to his own theory. A connected problem is that he never really enters a serious discussion with Marx on value – which is a term he seldom uses – and capital – which he indeed uses but does not actually develop theoretically. When Bourdieu theorises on capital (social, cultural, economic), he never argues how this capital can be set to work in the production-consumption process, how it is re-invested, etc. In fact, he seems to confuse value and capital in his theory: When he discusses capital in its three forms of appearance, he is actually speaking about value. In order for value to become capital, according to Marx, it has to be set in motion, ultimately producing surplus value or profit (which can then be reintroduced in the production-consumption circuit, producing again more value, and so on). When Bourdieu (1983/1986: 241) argues that 'capital is accumulated labor' this is a misconception of Marx, whose original statement holds that 'by incorporating living labour into their lifeless objectivity, the capitalist simultaneously transforms value. i.e. past labour in its objectified and lifeless form, into capital, value which can perform its own valorisation process' (Marx 1867/1976: 302). So, what Bourdieu really proposes, but fails to conceptually capture, is that the acquired abilities and dispositions that form a person's habitus, the accumulated labour objectified in the person in 'embodied form', is value rather than capital, and the process Bourdieu does not discuss is the valorisation process by which this value is turned into re-investable capital, that is, value set to work. By re-introducing the distinction between value and capital in the field model, we can also distinguish between values as standards, criteria or measures by which we also value agents in, for example, fields of consumption, and capital, as this value put to work in the process of valorisation that ultimately strives to produce surplus (for example, acquire a more elevated or legitimate position in the field of cultural consumption).

However, and given the bias of economic value in discussions of value in general, there is also a profound risk that the language adopted from the field of economy is counter-productive to the aims of Bourdieu's field analysis and his insistence on the autonomy of the various fields. Autonomy, to Bourdieu, is the founding basis for the generation of the field's specific value (or capital, as Bourdieu would say), the principles for its accumulation, and the specificities of its working in the field. And one can but wonder whether Bourdieu's choice of terminology, adopted from the sphere of economics, does not do exactly what he fears the most: subsuming every value form to the economic logic. If one wanted to be hard on Bourdieu one could say that he helps this process on the way by further confirming the idea that it is the economy in the last instance that is decisive.

One could, for example, play with the idea of what would happen if we reversed this argument. What if we adopted the terminology of the field of cultural production, the principles of valuation, and the logics of aesthetics in other fields, for example the field of the economy? If the logics of valuation from the market can be applied to fields of cultural production, could not also logics from cultural valuation be applied in the field of the economy? We never hear such proposals, whereas the opposite is repeatedly suggested. Why is this? Why are there so many voices arguing that the field of cultural production should be run according to principles of valuation from the market and the value logics that reside there? Why is the measure of success increasingly put in economic terms? Why is culture increasingly used as a technology to reach other ends? Because this is what we are witnessing today, in public discourse as well as in national cultural policy. In Sweden and elsewhere, cultural technologies are adopted to improve national export industries and many other areas of life.

It's Capitalism, Stupid!

At the beginning of this book I argued for the importance of acknowledging other forms of value than the economic. It will stand out as obvious that economic value in one way or another seeps back into the discussion, indeed into value itself in general. At a seminar a couple of years ago, when I presented some of the thoughts I have presented here, I got the laconic comment 'Well, it is called capitalism'. Well, it is. But what I hope to have accomplished is a more dynamic model for analysing media and culture production in late capitalism, the ways it works, and the various value forms that appear around, and are often drawn into, the production and reception processes.

As accounted for above, Bourdieu is often misunderstood as a fierce critic of fine arts production and cultural snobbery. This apprehension stems from a far too superficial reading of his work. One of the places in which he is most clear in regard to his position in relation to fields of cultural production is the 'normative' appendix 'For a Corporatism of the Universal' in *The Rules of Art* (Bourdieu 1992/1996: 337ff). In this normative call to fellow intellectuals, Bourdieu calls for a common commitment to 'defending the autonomy of the universes of cultural production' by insisting on control over 'the instruments of production and circulation (and hence of evaluation and consecration)' (p. 344). Through securing such control over 'the means of production' (as Marx would put it), the logic of evaluation remains in the autonomous field. Hence the logic that governs the field's specific value, and the forms it can appear in, is defended and uncontaminated by outer demand and pressures from forces of other fields (for example, the economic or the political).

With Bourdieu I too would like to join in a defence of the values produced in the fields of cultural production, and, for that matter, also in fields of knowledge production and the unquestioned autonomy that is the foundational basis for preserving these values. There is something deeply problematic in the fact that the basic measure of all social and cultural activities is concentrated to one value form. This is especially troublesome as this value form, adopted from economic worth, reduces all *qualitative* distinctions to *quantity* by forcing upon the aesthetic, social, political, cognitive and cultural fields the principles of equivalence and interchangeability.

In his discussion of the consequences of neoliberalism for voice, Nick Couldry holds voice as a 'second order' value, that is a 'value *about* values', a 'reflexive concern with the conditions for voice as a process' (Couldry 2010: 2). By analogy, I would say we also need to defend and protect values in the plural, which operate with different logics (not all of which are reducible to economic processes), have different impacts on our lives, and contribute to richer and more varied ways to live our cultures.

Bibliography

Adorno, T.W. 1941. On Popular Music. *Studies in Philosophy and Social Sciences*, 9, 17-48.

Adorno, T.W. 1967/1975. The Culture Industry Reconsidered. *New German Critique*, 6 (Autumn), 12-19.

Alasuutari, P. (ed.) 1999. *Rethinking the Media Audience*. London: Sage.

Anderson, C. 2006. *The Long Tail: Why the Future of Business is Selling Less of More*. New York: Hyperion.

Andersson, J. and Snickars, P. (eds) 2010. *Efter The Pirate Bay*. Stockholm: Kungliga Biblioteket.

Andrejevic, M. 2002. The Work of Being Watched. Interactive Media and the Exploitation of Self-disclosure, *Critical Studies in Media Communication*, 19(2), 230-48.

Andrejevic, M. 2007. *iSpy: Surveillance and Power in the Interactive Era*. Lawrence: University of Kansas Press.

Ang, I. 1982/1991. *Watching Dallas: Soap Opera and the Melodramatic Imagination*. London and New York: Routledge.

Ang, I. 1991. *Desperately Seeking the Audience*. London: Routledge.

Ang, I. and Hermes, J. 1991. Gender and/in Media Studies, in *Mass Media and Society*, edited by J. Curran and M. Gurevitch. London: Edward Arnold, 307-28.

Arvidsson, A. 2006. *Brands: Meaning and Value in Media Culture*. London and New York: Routledge.

Banks, J. and Humphreys, S. 2008. The Labour of User Co-Creators: Emergent Social Networks Markets, *Convergence*, 14(4), 401-18.

Barker, M. (ed.) 1984. *The Video Nasties: Freedom and Censorship in the Media*. London: Pluto Press.

Barnouw, E. 1978/1979. *The Sponsor: Notes on a Modern Potentate*. New York: Oxford University Press.

Barthes, R. 1971/1977. From Work to Text, in *Image – Music – Text*. London: Fontana, 155-64.

Baudrillard, J. 1968. *Le système des objets*. Paris: Gallimard.

Baudrillard, J. 1970/1998. *The Consumer Society: Myths and Structures*. London: Sage.

Baudrillard, J. 1972/1981. *For a Critique of the Political Economy of the Sign*. St. Louis: Telos.

Baudrillard, J. 1973/1975. *The Mirror of Production*. St. Louis: Telos.

Baudrillard, J. 1976/1993. *Symbolic Exchange and Death*. London: Sage.

Bauman, Z. 1998. *Work, Consumerism and the New Poor.* Buckingham: Open
    University Press.

Beniger, J. 1986. *The Control Revolution: Technological and Economic Origins of
    the Information Society.* Cambridge, MA: Harvard University Press.

Benjamin, Walter 1936/1977. The Work of Art in the Age of Mechanical
    Reproduction, in *Mass Communication and Society*, edited by J. Curran, M.
    Gurevitch and J. Wollacott. London: Edward Arnold, 384-408.

Benjamin, W. 1955/1999. Thesis on the Philosophy of History, in *Illuminations*.
    London: Pimlico.

Benjamin, W. 1982/1999. *The Archades Project.* Cambridge, MA: The Belknap
    Press.

Benkler, Y. 2006. *The Wealth of Networks: How Social Production Transforms
    Markets and Freedom.* New Haven and London: Yale University Press.

Benson, R. 1999. Field Theory in Comparative Context: A New Paradigm for
    Media Studies. *Theory and Society*, 28(3), 463-98.

Berger, A.A. 1992. *Popular Culture Genres: Theories and Texts.* Newbury Park,
    London and New Delhi: Sage.

Berland, J. 1990. Radio Space and Industrial Time: The Case of Music Formats.
    Popular Music, 9(2), 179-92.

Berman, M. 1982/1988. *All That is Solid Melts into Air: The Experience of
    Modernity.* New York: Penguin.

Blomqvist, U., Eriksson, L-E., Findahl, O., Selg, H. and Wallis, R. 2005. *Trends in
    Downloading and Filesharing of Music.* World Internet Institute. Available at:
    www.worldinternetinstitute.org [Last accessed 7 April 2006].

Blumler, J.G. 1979. The Role of Theory in Uses and Gratifications Studies.
    Communication Research, 6(1), 9-36.

Bolin, G. 1994a. Medieetnografiska kulturstudier. Metodologiska problem inom
    medieforskningen. *Kulturella perspektiv*, 3(4), 45-59.

Bolin, G. 1994b. Beware! Rubbish! Popular Culture and Strategies of Distinction.
    Young, 2(1), 33-49.

Bolin, G. 1994c. Vad är ett medium? En guide till 'Liftarens guide till galaxen',
    in *Kommunikationens korsningar*, edited by U. Carlsson, C. von Feilitzen, J.
    Fornäs, T. Holmqvist, S. Ross and H. Strand, Göteborg: Nordicom, 213-28.

Bolin, G. 1998. *Filmbytare: Videovåld, kulturell produktion och unga män.* Umeå:
    Boréa.

Bolin, G. 1999. Producing Cultures. The Construction of Forms and Contents of
    Contemporary Youth Cultures. *Young*, 7(1), 50-65.

Bolin, G. 2000. Film Swapping in the Public Sphere. Youth Audiences and
    Alternative Cultural Publicities. *Javnost/The Public*, 7(2), 57-73.

Bolin, G. 2002. In the Market for Symbolic Commodities. Swedish Lottery Game
    Show 'Bingolotto' and the Marketing of Social and Cultural Values. *Nordicom
    Review*, 23(1-2), 177-204.

Bolin, G. 2004a. Spaces of Television. The Structuring of Consumers in a Swedish
    Shopping Mall, in *Mediaspace: Place, Scale and Culture in a Media Age*,

edited by N. Couldry and A. McCarthy, London and New York: Routledge, 126-44.

Bolin, G. 2004b. The Value of Being Public Service. The Shifting of Power Relations in Swedish Television Production. *Media, Culture & Society*, 26(2), 277-87.

Bolin, G. 2005. Notes From Inside the Factory. The Production and Consumption of Signs and Sign Value in Media Industries. *Social Semiotics*, 15(3), 289-306.

Bolin, G. 2006. Visions of Europe. Cultural Technologies of Nation States. *International Journal of Cultural Studies*, 9(2), 189-206.

Bolin, G. 2009. Symbolic Production and Value in Media Industries. *Journal of Cultural Economy*, 2(3), 345-61.

Bolin, G. and Forsman, M. 2002. *Bingolotto: Produktion, Text, Reception.* Huddinge: Södertörn University.

Bolin, G. and Ståhlberg, P. 2010. Between Community and Commodity. Nationalism and Nation Branding, in *Communicating the Nation: National Topographies of Global Media Landscapes*, edited by A. Roosvall and I. Solivara Moring, Göteborg: Nordicom, 79-101.

Boltanski, L. and Thévenot, L. 1991/2006. *On Justification: Economies of Worth.* Princeton and Oxford: Princeton University Press.

Bourdieu, P. 1972/1992. *Outline of a Theory of Practice.* Cambridge: Cambridge University Press.

Bourdieu, P. 1977/1993. The Production of Belief: Contribution to an Economy of Symbolic Goods, in *The Field of Cultural Production: Essays on Art and Literature*, Cambridge: Polity Press, 74-111.

Bourdieu, P. 1979/1989. *Distinction: A Social Critique of the Judgement of Taste.* London: Routledge.

Bourdieu, P. 1980/1992. *The Logic of Practice.* Cambridge: Polity Press.

Bourdieu, P. 1983/1986. The Forms of Capital, in *Handbook of Theory and Research for the Sociology of Education*, edited by J.G. Richardson, New York: Greenwood Press, 241-58.

Bourdieu, P. 1983/1991. Did You Say 'Popular'?, in *Language and Symbolic Power*. Cambridge: Polity Press, 90-102.

Bourdieu, P. 1990. *In Other Words: Essays Towards a Reflexive Sociology.* Cambridge: Polity Press.

Bourdieu, P. 1991. *Language and Symbolic Power.* Cambridge: Polity Press.

Bourdieu, P. 1992/1996. *The Rules of Art: Genesis and Structure of the Literary Field.* Cambridge: Polity Press.

Bourdieu, P. 1993. *The Field of Cultural Production: Essays on Art and Literature.* Cambridge: Polity Press.

Bourdieu, P. 1996. *The State Nobility: Elite Schools in the Field of Power.* Cambridge: Polity Press.

Bourdieu, P. 1996/1998. *On Television and Journalism.* London: Pluto.

Bourdieu, P. and J-C. Passeron 1964/1979. *The Inheritors: French Students and Their Relation to Culture.* London: Routledge.

Bourdieu, P. and Wacquant, L.J.D. 1992. *An Invitation to Reflexive Sociology.* Cambridge: Polity Press.

Boyle, J. 2003. The Second Enclosure Movement and the Construction of the Public Domain. *Law and Contemporary Problems*, 66(1-2), 33-74.

Brabham, D.C. 2008. Crowdsourcing as a Model for Problem Solving. An Introduction and Cases. *Convergence*, 14(1), 75-90.

Broadcast 2006. BBC Develops Web Ratings System (6 October), 6.

Bruno, G. 1993. *Streetwalking on a Ruined Map: Cultural Theory and the City Films of Elvira Notari.* Princeton: Princeton University Press.

Bruns, A. 2006. Towards Produsage: Futures for User-Led Content Production, in *Proceedings: Cultural Attitudes towards Communication and Technology 2006*, edited by F. Sudweeks, H. Hrachovec and C. Ess, Perth: Murdoch University, 275-84.

Bruns, A. 2007. The Future Is User-Led: The Path towards Widespread Produsage. Paper presented at PerthDAC conference, Perth, Western Australia, 15-18 September. 2007.

Bruns, A. 2008. Reconfiguring Television for a Networked, Produsage Context. *Media International Australia*, 126, 82-94.

Bürger, P. 1974/1984. *Theory of the Avant-garde.* Minneapolis: University of Minnesota Press.

Burkart, P. and McCourt, T. 2006. *Digital Music Wars: Ownership and Control of the Celestial Jukebox.* Lanham: Rowman and Littlefield.

Burston, J. 2009. Recombinant Broadway. *Continuum*, 23(2), 159-69.

Caldwell, J.T. 2008. *Production Culture: Industrial Reflexivity and Critical Practice in Film and Television.* Durham and London: Duke University Press.

Castells, M. 1996. *The Information Age: Economy, Society and Culture, Part 1: The Rise of the Network Society.* Malden, MA Blackwell.

Cawelti, J.G. 1976. *Adventure, Mystery, and Romance: Formula Stories as Art and Popular Culture.* Chicago: University of Chicago Press.

Cohen, S. and Taylor, L. 1976/1992. *Escape Attempts: The Theory and Practice of Resistance to Everyday Life* (2nd edition). London and New York: Routledge.

Collins, J. 1989. *Uncommon Cultures: Popular Culture and Post-Modernism.* New York and London: Routledge.

Couldry, N. 2003. Media Meta-capital: Extending the Range of Bourdieu's Field Theory. *Theory and Society*, 32(5-6), 653-77.

Couldry, N. 2010. *Why Voice Matters: Culture and Politics after Neoliberalism.* London: Sage.

Cunningham, S. 2009. Trojan Horse or Rorschach Blot? Creative Industries Discourse Around the World. *Journal of Cultural Policy*, 15(4), 375-86.

Curran, J., Morley, D. and Walkerdine, V. (eds) 1996. *Cultural Studies and Communications.* London: Edward Arnold.

Denward, M. 2008. Broadcast Culture Meets Role-Playing Culture: Consequences for Audience Participation in a Cross-media Production. Paper presented to the IAMCR conference, Stockholm July 20-25.

Deuze, M. 2007. *Media Work*. Cambridge: Polity Press.

Deuze, M. 2009. Media Industries, Work and Life. *European Journal of Communication*, 24(4), 467-80.

Drotner, K. 1993. Medieetnografiske problemstillinger – en oversigt. *Mediekultur*, no. 21, 5-22.

Drotner, K. 2002. New Media, New Options, New Communities? Towards a Convergent Media and ICT Research. *Nordicom-Information*, 24(2-3), 11-22.

Durkheim, É. 1912/2001. *The Elementary Forms of Religious Life*. Oxford: Oxford University Press.

Dyer-Witheford, N. 1999. *Cyber-Marx: Cycles and Circuits of Struggle in High-Technology Capitalism*. Urbana and Chicago: University of Illinois Press.

Ellis, J. 1992. *Visible Fictions: Cinema, Television, Video* (2nd edition). London and New York: Routledge.

Elson, D. 1979. The Value Theory of Labour, in *Value: The Representation of Labour in Capitalism*, edited by D. Elson, London: CSE Books, 115-80.

Ericson, S. 2004. *Två drömspel: Från Strindbergs modernism till Potters television*. Stockholm/Stehag: Brutus Östlings Bokförlag Symposion.

Eysenck, H.J. and Nias, D.K.B. 1978/1980. *Sex, Violence and the Media*. Frogmore: Granada.

Fiske, J. 1987. *Television Culture*. London and New York: Routledge.

Fleischer, R. 2009. *Musikundret: Om 'Den Svenska Musikexporten' och arvet från 1990-talet*. unpublished paper. Available at: http://www.rasmusfleischer.se/forskning/ [Last accessed 31 January 2011].

Folbre, N. 1982. Exploitation Comes Home: A Critique of the Marxian Theory of Family Labour. *Cambridge Journal of Economics*, 6(4), 317-29.

Forsman, M. 2010. *Lokal radio i konkurrens 1975-2010: Utbud, publik och varumärken*. Stockholm: Ekerlids förlag.

Forsman, M. and Stiernstedt, F. 2006. The Decoding of a Format. Examples from Music Radio Production in Sweden and Estonia. *Recherches en communication*, no. 26, 45-61.

Fowler, B. 2006. Autonomy, Reciprocity and Science in the Thought of Pierre Bourdieu. *Theory, Culture & Society*, 23(6), 99-117.

Frith, S. 1988. Video Pop: Picking up the Pieces, in *Facing the Music*, edited by Simon Frith, New York: Pantheon, 88-130.

Frith, S. 1991. The Good, the Bad, and the Indifferent: Defending Popular Culture from the Populists. *Diacritics*, 21(4), 102-15.

Frow, J. 1995. *Cultural Studies and Cultural Value*. Oxford: Oxford University Press.

Gagnier, R. 2000. *The Insatiability of Human Wants: Economics and Aesthetics in Market Society*. Chicago and London: University of Chicago Press.

Gaines, J. 1990. Superman and the Protective Strength of the Trademark, in *Logics of Television: Essays in Cultural Criticism*, edited by Patricia Mellencamp, Bloomington and London: Indiana University Press/BFI, 173-92.

Galbraith, J.K. 1958/1964. *Överflödets samhälle*. Stockholm: Prisma.

Galbraith, J.K. 1969. The Shift of Power. Technology, Planning, and Organization, in *Values and the Future: The Impact of Technological Change on American Values*, edited by K. Baier and N. Rescher, New York: The Free Press, 555-67.

Galbraith, J.K. 1970. Economics as a System of Belief. *American Economic Review*, 60(2), 469-78.

Garnham, N. 1995. Political Economy and Cultural Studies: Reconciliation or Divorce?, *Critical Studies of Mass Communication* 12, 62-71.

Garnham, N. 2005. From Cultural to Creative Industries. *International Journal of Cultural Policy*, 11(1), 15-29.

Gendron, B. 1986. Theodor Adorno meets the Cadillacs, in *Studies in Entertainment: Critical Approaches to Mass Culture*, edited by Tania Modleski, Bloomington and Indianapolis: Indiana University Press, 18-36.

Genette, G. 1987/1997. *Paratexts: Thresholds of Interpretation*. Cambridge: Cambridge University Press.

Gillespie, M. 1995. *Television, Ethnicity and Cultural Change.* London and New York: Routledge.

Goggin, G. 2009. Adapting the Mobile Phone: The iPhone and Its Consumption. *Continuum*, 23(2), 231-44.

Gray, J. 2010. *Show Sold Separately: Promos, Spoilers, and Other Media Paratexts*. New York: New York University Press.

Guillory, J. 1993. *Cultural Capital: The Problem of Literary Canon Formation.* Chicago: University of Chicago Press.

Gustafsson, K.-E. 2009. Dagspressens affärsmodeller. *Ekonomiska samfundets tidskrift*, no. 1/2009, 23-8.

Hall, S. 1973. *Encoding/Decoding in the Television Discourse.* Stencilled occasional paper from CCCS no. 7, Birmingham: Birmingham University/ CCCS.

Hall, S. 1974/2003. Marx's Notes on Method: A 'Reading' of the '1857 Introduction'. *Cultural Studies*, 17(2), 113-49.

Hall, S. and Jefferson, T. (eds) 1976/1991. *Resistance Through Rituals: Youth Sub-cultures in Post-War Britain.* London: HarperCollins Academic.

Hannerz, U. 1992. *Cultural Complexity: Studies in the Social Organization of Meaning.* New York: Columbia University Press.

Hannerz, U. 2004. *Foreign News: Exploring the World of Foreign Correspondents.* Chicago: University of Chicago Press.

Hardt, M. 2005. Immaterial Labor and Artistic Production. *Rethinking Marxism*, 17(2), 175-7.

Hartley, J. (ed.) 2005. *Creative Industries*. Malden, MA: Blackwell.

Hartley, J. 2009. From the Consciousness Industry to the Creative Industries: Consumer-Created Content, Social Network Markets, and the Growth of Knowledge, in *The Media Industry Studies Book*, edited by J. Holt and A. Perren, Malden, MA: Blackwell, 231-44.

Harvey, D. 2003. *The New Imperialism*. Oxford: Oxford University Press.

Haug, W.F. 1971/1986. *Critique of Commodity Aesthetics: Appearance, Sexuality and Advertising in Capitalist Society.* Minneapolis: University of Minnesota Press.

Hemmungs Wirtén, E. 2008. *Terms of Use: Negotiating the Jungle of the Intellectual Commons.* Toronto: Toronto University Press.

Herman, E.S. and McChesney, R.W. 1997. *The Global Media: The New Missionaries of Corporate Capitalism.* London and Washington: Cassell.

Hesmondhalgh, D. 2006. Bourdieu, the Media and Cultural Production. *Media, Culture & Society,* 28(2), 211-31.

Hesmondhalgh, D. 2007. *The Cultural Industries* (second edition). London: Sage.

Hesmondhalgh, D. and Pratt, A.C. 2005. Cultural Industries and Cultural Policy. *International Journal of Cultural Policy,* 11(1), 1-13.

Hill, A. 2005. *Reality TV.* London and New York: Routledge.

Hill, A. 2007. *Restyling Factual TV: The Reception of News, Documentary and Reality Genres.* London and New York: Routledge.

Hills, M. 2002. *Fan Cultures.* London and New York: Routledge.

Hoggart, R. 1957/1958. *The Uses of Literacy: Aspects of Working-Class Life With Special Reference to Publications and Entertainments.* Harmondsworth: Penguin.

Horkheimer, M. and Adorno, T.W. 1947/1994. The Culture Industry: Enlightenment as Mass Deception in *Dialectic of Enlightenment,* New York: Continuum.

Howard, P.N. 2007. Testing the Leap-Frog Hypothesis: The Impact of Existing Infrastructure and Telecommunications Policy on the Global Digital Divide. *Information, Communication & Society,* 10(2), 133-57.

Humphreys, E. (ed.) 2008. *International Copyright and Intellectual Property Law: Challanges for Media Content Producers.* Jönköping: Jönköping International Business School.

Humphreys, E. 2011. *Programformat och medier i konvergens: Formathandel, juridiskt skydd och branschpraxis.* Göteborg: Nordicom.

Huyssen, A. 1986. *After the Great Divide: Modernism, Mass Culture and Post-modernism.* Houndmills and London: Macmillan.

Innis, H. 1951. *The Bias of Communication.* Toronto: University of Toronto Press.

International Telecommunications Union 2010. *The World in 2010.* Available at: http://www.itu.int/ITU-D/ict/material/FactsFigures2010.pdf [Last accessed 22 October 2010].

Jakobsson, P. and Stiernstedt, F. 2010. Pirates of Silicon Valley. State of Exception and Dispossession in Web 2.0. *First Monday,* 15(7), Available at: http://firstmonday.org/htbin/cgiwrap/bin/ojs/index.php/fm/article/view/2799/2577 [Last accessed 20 January 2011].

Jameson, F. 1981. *The Political Unconscious: Narrative as a Socially Symbolic Act.* Ithaca, NY: Cornell University Press.

Jenkins, H. 1992. *Textual Poachers: Television Fans and Participatory Culture.* New York and London: Routledge.

Jenkins, H. 2006. *Convergence Culture: Where Old and New Media Collide*. New York: New York University Press.

Jenkins, H. 2007. *Tranmedia Storytelling 101*, available at: www.henryjenkins. org/2007/03/transmedia_storytelling_101.html [Last accessed 29 September 2009].

Jensen, J.F. 1998. Communication Research after the Mediasaurus?. *Nordicom Review*, 19(1), 39-52.

Jensen, K.B. 2010. *Media Convergence: The Three Degrees of Network, Mass, and Interpersonal Communication*. London and New York: Routledge.

Jhally, S. and Livant, B. 1986. Watching as Working: The Valorization of Audience Consciousness. *Journal of Communication*, 36(3), 124-43.

Jowett, G.S., Jarvie, I.C. and Fuller, K.H. 1996. *Children and the Movies: Media Influence and the Payne Fund Controversy*. Cambridge: Cambridge University Press.

Joyce, J. 1922/1946. *Ulysses*. New York: Random House.

Kenney, M. 1997. Value-Creation in the Late Twentieth Century: The Rise of the Knowledge Worker, in *Cutting Edge: Technology, Information Capitalism and Social Revolution*, eds, J. Davies, T. Hirsch and M. Stock. London: Verso, 87-102.

Kjus Y. 2006. Når publikum blir produsenter. Deltakelse i det kommersielle underholdningsformatet Idol. *Norsk medietidsskrift*, 13(3), 220-41.

Kracauer, S. 1927/1995. The Mass Ornament, in *The Mass Ornament: Weimar Essays*. Cambridge, MA: Harvard University Press, 75-88.

Kretschmer, M. and Kawohl, F. 2004. The History and Philosophy of Copyright, in *Music and Copyright*, edited by S. Frith and L. Marshall. Edinburgh: Edinburgh University Press, 21-53.

Kretschmer, M., Klimis, G.M. and Wallis, R. 2001. Music in Electronic Markets: An Empirical Study. *New Media & Society*, 3(4), 417-41.

Laermans, R. 1992. The Relative Rightness of Pierre Bourdieu: Some Sociological Comments on the Legitimacy of Postmodern Art, Literature and Culture. *Cultural Studies*, 6(2), 248-60.

Lagerkvist, A. 2009. Transitional Times. 'New Media' – Novel Histories and Trajectories. *Nordicom Review*, 30(1), 3-18.

Larsson, S. 2005/2009. *The Girl With the Dragon Tattoo*. London: Quercus Books.

Lash, S. and Urry, J. 1994. *Economies of Sign and Space*. London: Sage.

Lash, S. and Lury, C. 2007. *Global Culture Industry: The Mediation of Things*. Cambridge: Polity Press.

Lazarsfeld, P.F. 1961. Mass Culture Today, in *Culture for the Millions? Mass Media in Modern Society*, edited by N. Jacobs, Boston: Beacon Press, ix-xxv.

Lazzarato, M. 1996. Immaterial Labor, in *Radical Thought in Italy: A Potential Politics*, edited by P. Virno and H. Hardt, Minneapolis: University of Minnesota Press, 133-50.

Le Bon, G. 1896/2006. *The Crowd: A Study of the Popular Mind*. New York: Cosimo Classics.

Lessig, L. 2003. The Creative Commons. *Florida Law Review*, 55, 763-77.

Lessig, L. 2004. *Free Culture: The Nature and Future of Creativity*. New York: Penguin.

Lessig, L. 2008. *Remix: Making Art and Commerce Thrive in the Hybrid Economy*. New York: Penguin.

Lewis, L.A. (ed.) 1992. *The Adoring Audience: Fan Culture and Popular Media*. New York and London: Routledge.

Liebes, T. and Katz, E. 1990/1993. *The Export of Meaning: Cross-cultural Readings of Dallas*. Cambridge: Polity Press.

Löwenfeldt, J. 2009. Hollywood nästa för The Company P *it24*, 25 February, Available at: http://www.idg.se/2.1085/1.214427/hollywood-nasta-for-the-company-p, [Last accessed 23 December 2010].

Lowenthal, L. 1950/1957. Historical perspectives of popular culture, in *Mass Culture: The Popular Arts in America*, edited by B. Rosenberg and D.M. White, New York: The Free Press, 46-58.

Lowenthal, L. 1961. *Literature, Popular Culture and Society*. Englewood Cliffs, NJ: Prentice-Hall.

Lucas, H.C. 1999. *Information Technology and the Productivity Paradox: The Search for Value*. New York: Oxford University Press.

Lüders, M. 2008. Conceptualizing Personal Media. *New Media & Society*, 10(5), 683-702.

Lüders, M., Pröitz, L. and Rasmussen, T. (eds) 2007. *Personlige medier: Livet mellom skjermene*. Oslo: Gyldendal.

Luhmann, N. 1996/2000. *The Reality of the Mass Media*. Cambridge: Polity Press.

Lull, J. 1980/1990. The Social Uses of Television, in *Inside Family Viewing: Ethnographic Research on Television's Audiences*. London: Routledge, 28-48.

Lury, C. 2004. *Brands: The Logos of the Global Economy*. London and New York: Routledge.

Lynd, R.S. and Lynd, H.M. 1929. *Middletown: A Study in American Culture*. New York: Harcourt, Brace and Company.

Macdonald, D. 1953/1957. A Theory of Mass Culture, in *Mass Culture: The Popular Arts in America*, edited by B. Rosenberg and D.M. White, New York: The Free Press, 59-73.

Magendanz, D. 2003. Conflict and Complexity in Value Theory. *The Journal of Value Inquiry*, 37, 443-53.

Maltin, L. 1993. *Movie and Video Guide*. New York: Penguin/Signet.

Marvin, C. 1988/1995. Early Uses of the Telephone, in *Communication in History: Technology, Culture, Society*, edited by D. Crowley and P. Heyer, White Plains, NY: Longman, 173-82.

Marx, K. 1867/1976. *Capital: A Critique of Political Economy: Volume One*. London: Penguin Books.

Marx, K. 1932/1995. Den tyska ideologin, in *Människans frigörelse*, Göteborg: Daidalos, 135-98.

Marx, K. 1939/1993. *Grundrisse: Foundations of the Critique of Political Economy (Rough Draft)*. London: Penguin Books.

Marx, K. 1852/1971. *Louis Bonapartes 18: e brumaire*. Stockholm: Arbetarkultur.

Marx, K. and Engels, F. 1848/1888. *Manifesto for the Communist Party*, Marx/ Engels Internet Archive, Available at: www.marxists.org/archive/marx/ works/1848/communist-manifesto/ [Last accessed 2 December 2010].

Mauss, M. 1925/1990. *The Gift: The Form and Reason for Exchange in Archaic Societies*. London: Routledge.

Maxwell, R. 2001. Political Economy within Cultural Studies, in *A Companion to Cultural Studies*, edited by T. Miller, Oxford and Cambridge: Blackwell, 116-38.

McLuhan, M. 1964. *Understanding Media: The Extensions of Man*. New York: McGraw-Hill.

McRobbie, A. 1980. Settling Accounts with Subcultures. A Feminist Critique. *Screen Education*, no. 34: 37-49.

McQuail, D. 1997. *Audience Analysis*. Thousand Oaks: Sage.

Meehan, E.R. 1984. Ratings and the Institutional Approach: A Third Answer to the Commodity Question. *Critical Studies in Mass Communication*, 1(2), 216-25.

Meehan, E.R. 2000. Leisure or Labor?: Fan Ethnography and Political Economy, in *Consuming Audiences? Production and Reception in Media Research*, edited by I. Hagen and J. Wasko, Creskill, NJ: Hampton Press, 71-92.

Merrin, W. 2005. *Baudrillard and the Media*. Cambridge: Polity Press.

Miège, B. 1979. The Cultural Commodity. *Media, Culture & Society*, 1(3), 297-311.

Miller, D. 1995. Consumption as the Vanguard of History. A Polemic Way of an Introduction, in *Acknowledging Consumption: A Review of New Studies*, edited by D. Miller, London and New York: Routledge, 1-57.

Miller, T., Govill, N., McMurria, J. and Maxwell, R. 2001. *Global Hollywood*. London: BFI.

Moran, A. 1998. *Copycat Television: Globalisation, Program Formats and Cultural Identity*. Luton: University of Luton Press.

Moran, A. 2004. Television Formats in the World/The World of Television Formats, in *Television Across Asia: Television Industries, Programme Formats and Globalisation*, edited by A. Moran and M. Keane, London and New York: RoutledgeCurzon, 1-8.

Moran, A. and Keane, M. 2006. Cultural Power in International TV Format Markets. *Continuum: Journal of Media & Cultural Studies*, 20(1), 71-86.

Morley, D. 1986. *Family Television: Cultural Power and Domestic Leisure*. London and New York: Routledge.

Morley, D. 1992. *Television, Audiences and Cultural Studies*. London and New York: Routledge.

Morley, D. 1995. Theories of Consumption in Media Studies, in *Acknowledging Consumption: A Review of New Studies*, edited by Daniel Miller, London and New York: Routledge, 293-324.

Morley, D. 1997. Theoretical Orthodoxies: Textualism, Constructivism and the 'New Ethnography' in *Cultural Studies in Question*, edited by M. Ferguson and P. Golding, London: Sage, 121-37.

Mosco, V. 1996. *The Political Economy of Communication*. London: Sage.

Mosco, V. and Kaye, L. 2000. Questioning the Concept of the Audience, in *Consuming Audiences? Production and Reception in Media Research*, edited by I. Hagen and J. Wasko, Creskill, NJ: Hampton Press, 31-46.

Murdock, G. 2000. Peculiar Commodities: Audiences at Large in the World of Goods, in *Consuming Audiences? Production and Reception in Media Research*, edited by I. Hagen and J. Wasko, Creskill, NJ: Hampton Press, 47-70.

Neale, S. 1980. *Genre*. London: BFI.

Neale, S. 1990. Questions of Genre. *Screen*, 31(1), 45-66.

Negroponte, N. 1995/1996. *Being Digital*. New York: Vintage Books.

Nordenstreng, K. 1977. *Kommunikationsteori: Om massmedierna och kunskapsprocessen i samhället*. Stockholm: AWE/Gebers.

Oberholzer-Gee, F. and Strumpf, K. 2007. The Effect of File Sharing on Record Sales. An Empirical Analysis. *Journal of Political Economy*, 115(1), 1-42.

Ong, W. 1982. *Orality and Literacy: The Technologizing of the Word*. London: Methuen.

Ortega y Gasset, J. 1930/1964. *The Revolt of the Masses*. New York and London: Allen & Unwin.

Perason, R. 2008. The Jekyll and Hyde of Transmedia Storytelling. Paper presented to the conference Television and the Digital Public Sphere, Université de Paris II, Paris, France, 22-24 October.

Peters, J.D. 1999. *Speaking into the Air: A History of the Idea of Communication*. Chicago: University of Chicago Press.

Peters, J.D. 2003. The Subtlety of Horkheimer and Adorno: Reading 'The Culture Industry', in *Canonic Texts in Media Research*, edited by E. Katz, J.D. Peters, T. Liebes and A. Orloff, Cambridge: Polity Press, 58-73.

Pool, I. de S. 1983. *Technologies of Freedom: On Free Speech in an Electronic Age*. Cambridge, MA: Harvard University Press.

Qvist, P.O. 1994. 'Med svensk film ha de ingenting att göra'. Om en kort och expansiv period i svensk filmhistoria. *Filmhäftet*, 22(1), 40-7.

Radnoti, S. 1981. Mass culture. *Telos* 48, 27-47.

Radway, J. 1984/1987. *Reading the Romance*. London and New York: Verso.

Rasmussen, T. 2007. Nettverksintegrasjon og personlige medier, in *Personlige medier: Livet mellom skjermene*, edited by M. Lüders, L. Pröitz, T. Rasmussen, Oslo: Gyldendal, 247-69.

Riesman, D. (with N. Glaser and R. Denney) 1950/1955. *The Lonely Crowd: A Study in the Changing American Character* (abridged by the authors). New York: Doubleday Anchor Books.

Ritzer, G. 1999. *Enchanting a Disenchanted World: Revolutionizing the Means of Consumption*. Thousand Oaks: Sage.

Robb, D. 2004. *Operation Hollywood: How the Pentagon Shapes and Censors the Movies*. Amherst, NY: Prometheus Books.

Rosén, J. 2008. Copyright Control in Sweden and Internet Uses: File Sharer's Heaven or Not?, in *International Copyright and Intellectual Property Law: Challenges for Media Content Producers*, edited by E. Humphreys, Jönköping: Media Management and Transformation Centre, 29-42.

Rosenberg, B. and White, D.M. (eds) 1957. *Mass Culture: The Popular Arts in America*. New York: The Free Press/Macmillan.

Ross, A. 2000. The Mental Labor Problem. *Social Text*, 18(2), 1-31.

Rothenbuhler, E. and Dimmick, J. 1982. Popular Music: Concentration and Diversity in the Industry. *Journal of Communication*, 32(1), 143-9.

Schuback, M. sá C. and Ruin, H. (eds) 2006. *The Past's Present: Essays on the Historicity of Philosophical Thinking*. Huddinge: Södertörn.

Seaman, W.R. 1992. Active audience theory: Pointless populism. *Media, Culture & Society*, vol 14, 301-11.

Shils, E. 1961. Mass Society and Its Culture, in *Culture for the Millions? Mass Media in Modern Society*, edited by N. Jacobs, Boston: Beacon Press, 1-27.

Silverstone, R. 1994. *Television and Everyday Life*. London and New York: Routledge.

Silverstone, R. and Hirsch, E. (eds) 1992/1994. *Consuming Technologies: Media and Information in Domestic Spaces*. London and New York: Routledge.

Skoglund E. 1971. *Filmcensuren*. Stockholm: Pan/Norstedts.

Smith, A. 1776/1991. *The Wealth of Nations*. New York: Alfred A. Knopf.

Smythe, D. 1977 Communications: Blindspot of Western Marxism. *Canadian Journal of Political and Social Theory*, 1(3), 1-27.

Steemers, J. 2004. *Selling Television: British Television in the Global Marketplace*. London: BFI.

Sterne, J. 1997. Sounds Like the Mall of America: Programmed Music and the Architechtonics of Commercial Space. *Ethnomusicology*, 41(1), 22-50.

Stiernstedt, F. 2008. Maximising the Power of Entertainment. The Audience Commodity in Contemporary Radio. *The Radio Journal*, 6(2-3), 113-27.

Storsul, T. and Stuedal, D. (eds) 2007. *Ambivalence Towards Convergence: Digitalization and Media Change*. Göteborg: Nordicom.

Straubhaar, J. 1991. Beyond Media Imperialism. Assymetrical Interdependence and Cultural Proximity. *Critical Studies in Mass Communication*, 8(1), 39-59.

Straubhaar, J. 2000. Culture, Language and Social Class in the Globalization of Television, in *The New Communications Landscape: Demystifying Media Globalization*, edited by G. Wang, J. Servaes and A. Goonasekera, London and New York: Routledge, 199-224.

Streeter, T. 1996. *Selling the Air: A Critique of the Policy of Commercial Broadcasting in the United States*. Chicago and London: University of Chicago Press.

Strindberg, A. 1907/2010. *Black Banners: Genre Scenes from the Turn of the Century*. New York: Peter Lang.

Svensk Filmografi 3, 1930-1939. 1979. Stockholm: Svenska filminstitutet.

Terranova, T. 2000. Free Labor: Producing Culture for the Digital Economy. *Social Text*, 18(2), 33-58.

Thebérge, P. 1997. *Any Sound You Can Imagine: Making Music/Consuming Technology*. Hanover, NH: Wesleyan University Press.

Thompson, J.B. 1991. Editor's Introduction, in Bourdieu, P. *Language and Symbolic Power*, Cambridge: Polity Press, 1-31.

Thompson, J.B. 1995. *The Media and Modernity: A Social Theory of the Media*: Cambridge: Polity Press.

Turow, J. 2006. *Niche Envy: Marketing Discrimination in the Digital Age*. Cambridge, MA: MIT Press.

van Couvering, E. 2008. The History of the Internet Search Engine: Navigational Media and the Traffic Commodity. *Information Science and Knowledge Management*, 14, 177-206.

Vincendeau, G. 1988. Hollywood Babel: The Coming of Sound and the Multiple Language Version. *Screen*, 29(2), 24-39.

Virno, P. 1996. Notes on the General Intellect, in *Marxism Beyond Marxism*, edited by S. Makdisi, C. Casarino and R.E. Karl, London: Routledge, 265-72.

Waisbord, S. 2004. McTV. Understanding the Global Popularity of Television Formats. *Television & New Media*, 5(4), 359-83.

Wallis, R., Baden-Fuller, C., Kretschmer, M. and Klimis, G.M. 1999. Contested Collective Property Rights in Music. The Challenge of Principles of Reciprocity and Solidarity. *European Journal of Communication*, 14(1), 5-35.

Wardrip-Fruin, N. and Montfort, N. 2003. *The New Media Reader.* Cambridge, MA: MIT Press.

Wasko, J. 1994. *Hollywood in the Information Age: Beyond the Silver Screen*. Cambridge: Polity Press.

Web Analytics Association 2010. MMS Selects Nedstat for WebTV Measurement. Available at: http://www.webanalyticsassociation.org/news/43059/Vendor-MMS-selects-Nedstat-for-webTV-measurement.htm [Last accessed 21 January 2011].

Webster, J.G. and Phalen, P.F. 1997. *The Mass Audience: Rediscovering the Dominant Model*. Mahwah, NJ: Lawrence Erlbaum.

Widestedt, K. 2001. *Ett tongivande förnuft: Musikkritik i dagspress under två sekler*. Stockholm: Stockholm University.

Wikström, P. 2006. *Reluctantly Virtual: Modelling Copyright Industry Dynamics*. Karlstad: Karlstad University.

Wikström, P. 2009. *The Music Industry*. Cambridge: Polity Press.

Wilken, R. and Sinclair, J. 2010. 'Waiting for the Kiss of Life'. Mobile Media and Advertising. *Convergence*, 15(4), 427-45.

Williams, L. 1995. Bilder av rörelse. Kroppar, njutning, genrer. *Filmhäftet*, 23(4), 5-12.

Williams, R. 1958/1963. *Culture and Society 1780-1950.* Harmondsworth: Penguin.

Williams, R. 1961/1965. *The Long Revolution.* Harmondsworth: Penguin.

Williams, R. 1976. *Keywords.* London: Fontana.

Williams, R. 1979. *Politics and Letters: Interview with New Left Review.* London: Verso.

Willis, P. 1990. *Common Culture: Symbolic Work at Play in the Everyday Cultures of the Young.* Milton Keynes: Open University Press.

Wright, C.R. 1959. *Mass Communication: A Sociological Perspective.* New York: Random House.

Ytreberg, E. 2000. Continuity in Environments. The Evolution of Basic Practices and Dilemmas in Nordic Television Scheduling. *European Journal of Communication*, 17(3), 283-304.

Ytreberg, E. 2001. *Programskjemaarbeid i NRK Fjernsynet: Beslutningsprocesser i et maktsentrum* (National report for the Nordic Project 'Scheduling in Nordic public service television'). Oslo: Department of Media and Communication.

Ziehe, T. 1982/1986. *Ny ungdom: Om ovanliga läroprocesser.* Stockholm: Norstedts.

Zimmermann, P.R. 1995. *Reel Families: A Social History of Amateur Film.* Bloomington and Indianapolis: Indiana University Press.

Index